THE APOCALYPSE OF
THE RELUCTANT GNOSTICS

THE APOCALYPSE OF THE RELUCTANT GNOSTICS
Carl G. Jung and Philip K. Dick

Stuart Douglas

Routledge
Taylor & Francis Group

LONDON AND NEW YORK

First published 2018
by Routledge
2 Park Square, Milton Park, Abingdon, Oxon OX14 4RN

and by Routledge
711 Third Avenue, New York, NY 10017

Routledge is an imprint of the Taylor & Francis Group, an informa business

British Library Cataloguing-in-Publication Data
A catalogue record for this book is available from the British Library

Library of Congress Cataloging-in-Publication Data
A catalog record has been requested for this book

ISBN: 978-1-78220-607-1 (pbk)

Typeset in Palatino LT Std
by Medlar Publishing Solutions Pvt Ltd, India

MIX
Paper from
responsible sources
FSC   FSC® C013056
www.fsc.org

Printed and bound in Great Britain by
TJ International Ltd, Padstow, Cornwall

apocalypse

noun
1. any of a class of Jewish or Christian writings ... that were assumed to make revelations of the ultimate divine purpose.
2. a prophetic revelation esp. concerning a cataclysm in which the forces of good triumph over the forces of evil.
3. **any revelation or prophecy.**
4. any universal or widespread destruction or disaster.

origin
from Greek *apokálypsis*, from *apokalýptein* revelation, to uncover, to reveal (*apo-* + *kalýptein* to cover, conceal) + *-sis*.

CONTENTS

LIST OF FIGURES

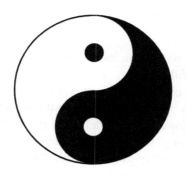

PREFACE

I go into an old church in the town I grew up in. I'm looking for a mission card (i.e., a card with my "mission" written on it) for the next phase of my life. I expect to find it on a window sill on the left-hand side. I find it where I was expecting, however I am a little surprised, and think: "This is real!" The mission card is about the size of a playing card, but the print is very small. I scan down the card and the only words that I can manage to read are, "Carl Jung". I ask a young woman if she can read what is on the card. She is about to do this when, distracted by an external noise, I wake up …

(Author's dream journal, July 2015)

In the closing remarks of my first book, *White Bird, Black Serpent, Red Book,* I noted that Jung had admitted that he felt that he had failed in what he considered to be his principal task: to awaken people to the fact that they have a soul, which he likened to a treasure buried in a field. I suggested that there was no failure on Jung's part, rather, the failure was on the part of others for not having fully realised what his life's work was really all about. I concluded that it now fell to others, particularly those who resonate with the Gnostic worldview on which his psychology is founded, to continue Jung's unfinished project. At that time, I did not feel that I would be among them. I thought my exploration of

Jung's work, and in particular, its Gnostic heritage, was complete, and I could move on to other things. Little did I realise, I would feel called to participate in the continuation of his unfinished project. This dream certainly suggests as much, and the present work is the result.

In Jung's psychology, the completion of psychological development and the attainment of psychological wholeness requires the reconciliation and integration of all opposites within the psyche. In my first book, I had commented that there was nothing more crucial to the salvation of humanity in our time than the restoration of the long-suppressed feminine principle. Only once the feminine has been restored as co-equal with the male principle can the integration of the male-female polarity occur. According to Jung, the equality of the feminine principle necessitates not simply the equality of women, but an actual equivalence of the feminine principle in its entirety, not only psychologically and spiritually, but also in a way that anchors the feminine in the figure of a divine woman in the same way that the divine masculine is represented in the figure of Christ (for Christians). He dismissed the notion of the Church as a symbol of the feminine as an intellectual abstraction and called for a personal figure. For the Gnostics, that figure is Sophia. In Gnostic philosophy, the soul, the daughter of Sophia, needs to be regenerated and restored to her rightful place in order to achieve the "resurrection from the dead". Christians talk about a second coming of Christ. If there is to be a second coming, and there needs to be, then, for the Gnostics, she will come as Sophia, because Christ and Sophia are one, and it is Sophia that has been neglected and must now be restored. Jung's Gnostic heritage permeates his life's work, and his unfinished project is nothing other than the restoration of Sophia. This book aims to make its contribution to that task.

At the start of this project, I had in mind a very different treatment of the subject. However, I had recently finished reading *The Exegesis of Philip K. Dick*, the personal journey of the American science-fiction author, and was struck by the parallels that existed between his and Jung's respective works. These parallels are examined in this book, but, in brief, both Jung and Dick had mystical or paranormal visions that they spent the rest of their lives trying to fathom and articulate. The essence of both their visions is undeniably Gnostic. Intrigued by the parallels, all the more so given that two very different people had articulated curiously similar visions from radically different perspectives, I felt compelled to attempt a modern retelling of the Gnostic myth in the light of their Gnostic visions. The pull was too great to resist. However, despite their respective visions being fundamentally Gnostic, they were both less than enthusiastic about accepting this. Throughout his career, Jung publicly denied he was Gnostic—or any other kind of mystic—despite his psychology being, without question, founded on his Gnostic vision, whereas, Dick, admitting that his vision was Gnostic, added that he was "not happy about it". Hence, the reluctant Gnostics.

In its exploration of the Gnostic visions of Jung and Dick, this book involves an investigation of the their personal journals, *The Red Book* and *The Exegesis of Philip K. Dick* respectively, which are, first and foremost, their individual odysseys to reclaim their lost, or neglected, souls. In other words, their attempts to restore Sophia within their own lives, since the soul is the daughter of Sophia. More accurately, perhaps, the soul *is* Sophia insofar as she manifests in the individual psyche. Whereas the main objective of this book is to present a modern reframing of the Gnostic tradition in the light of the Gnostic visions of Jung and Dick, it became evident, during the course of its writing, that it is fundamentally about the reclamation of soul, the restoration of Sophia, and that quest's crucial place in Gnostic soteriology.

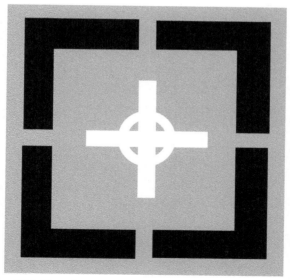

Figure 1. The Old Church.

The dream takes place in the old church in the town where I grew up. This represents where my spiritual life is at home, and that is, in the ancient Gnostic tradition. The church in question is situated in the centre of its roughly square cemetery which has, from memory, four gates leading into it. I chose to illustrate this dream with a plan view of this church represented in mandala form (Figure 1) to symbolise the wholeness I seek in it. I had this dream around the time I left a former career and was contemplating my vocation for the next phase of my life. This dream made it clear: my mission, should I choose to accept it, is to promote Jung's work, not as a form of psychotherapy, or as a process of psychological development, but as a modern day praxis of the ancient tradition of the Gnostics. Hopefully this book will not self-destruct in five seconds …

* * *

CHAPTER ONE

Introduction

People in the West are suffering from a chronic spiritual malaise. For a great many, their traditional religious institutions are failing to provide the authentic connection to the divine that their adherents yearn for. For the majority, this means Christianity which, numerically, is the dominant religious tradition in the West. For some, its doctrines have ossified into mere dogma and its rituals have, for the most part, become perfunctory, performed by rote and devoid of meaning. This disaffection that so many modern people in the West have for Christianity has been succinctly expressed by the Swiss psychologist, C. G. Jung in that the spiritually "dead" have returned from Jerusalem unsatisfied at having failed to find what they went there to look for. Whether these institutions are in terminal decline or can resurrect themselves remains to be seen.

The Church's failures are legion and this has elicited a number of responses from those who might otherwise be considered, nominally at least, as Christian. First, there are those who have disavowed Western religion, and any form of spirituality for that matter, altogether. Nature abhors a vacuum, however, and something, anything, usually rampant materialism in one form another, will rush to fill the void. Consequently, for these apostates, the new gods have become success and excess,

1

fame—occasionally one's own, but more often sought vicariously through the lives of the latest "celebrities"—and fortune, sex, drugs, and rock n' roll, and the futile quest for the fountain of eternal youth. In the cult motion picture, *Trainspotting* (the original, Macdonald, 1996), the leading protagonist, Renton, narrates a withering attack on this modern, secular life that the spiritually disenfranchised all too often succumb to; a life dedicated to the pursuit of career and fixed-interest mortgage repayments, the latest must-have "mod cons", such as over-sized televisions and electrical kitchen appliances, and trendy designer wear with matching accessories. In other words, an empty, meaning-less life that leaves people wondering who they really are, distracted by the latest mind-numbing, spirit-crushing game shows on the televi-sion while gorging themselves on junk food, all of which leads, inexo-rably, to its fateful conclusion, a soul-destroying demise, in which life seeps steadily out of them as they see out their days in a miserable nursing home.

Second, there are others who have similarly turned their back on the Church of their birth but have, instead, looked elsewhere for spiri-tual nourishment; a response pithily summed up in the bumper-sticker witticism that people are leaving the Church and turning back to God. Indeed, I suspect that God has probably left the Church as well. Could the last person to leave put the lights out. Of these, a great many since the counterculture movement of the 1960s have looked to the East to fill the gaping void, seeking refuge in the Three Jewels of Buddhism, the Buddha, the Dharma, and the Sangha, pursuing *darshan* from an enlightened master, or practising one of the Yogic paths with its prom-ise of union with the divine.

Yet another group have sought to fill the gnawing emptiness by turning to one (or more) of the distinct, but related, range of movements which, together, comprise what is generally referred to as the Western Esoteric Tradition or, its variant and companion, the Western Mystical Tradition. These traditions include Neoplatonism, Hermeticism, Kabbalah, Alchemy, Rosicrucianism, Freemasonry, Theosophy, Mystical Christianity, Esoteric Christianity, Neopaganism, and Wicca, to name only a few. Many, if not all, of these traditions have been deemed hereti-cal at one time or another in their history, by the Christian Church and suppressed—often brutally so. However, the essence of their teachings has never really gone away, but simply been forced into what has been described as an underground river, only to resurface at a later time, in a different form. Whether this river represents an uninterrupted chain from the present era all the way back to antiquity, or whether these heterogeneous movements are discrete, but related, instances of the same spiritual essence emerging anew from the depths of the collective unconscious, is perhaps moot. Former rock musician and now full-time writer on the Western Mystery Tradition, Gary Lachman (2015) suggests that, for the most part, this underground river remains "like a hidden spring at which a few daring souls [take] refreshment" (loc. 3158). One significant tributary of this mighty underground river, which has recently resurfaced with some vigour, is what is generally, if rather loosely, referred to as *Gnosticism*. The work of two daring souls who have drunk at the Gnostic well are the principal focus of this book.

* * *

What is Gnosticism? It is a modern term used to denote a collection of ancient spiritual traditions, generally syncretic in nature, with historical roots extending at least as far back as Plato and Second Temple Judaism. If a religion is defined to be a system of doctrines and practices—typically grounded in, and inextricably linked to, a particular culture—which is concerned with humanity's relationship with the divine, then, to the extent that Gnosticism might be considered to be a religion, it is somewhat akin to Hinduism insofar as it is a rather diverse family of related traditions. Given the diversity within the movement, it is of no surprise that Gnosticism means different things to different people, and the gamut of definitions that have been used for the term "Gnosticism" is broad; perhaps too broad. On the one hand, at the more precisely defined end of the spectrum, the term is typically used—inaccurately it might be added—to refer to a group of Christian heresies which arose in the second century of the Common Era and flourished for a few centuries, before being extinguished. There are some scholars (e.g., Brakke, 2010) who suggest an even more specific definition in which the term is reserved to refer exclusively to a particular sect within Gnosticism known as the Sethians. At the other, "looser" end of the spectrum, we have the New Agers who, as is their wont, have appropriated the term to mean … well, just about anything they want it to mean. Other scholars (e.g., Williams, 1996) have questioned the term's value altogether and have gone as far as to suggest abandoning it as a dubious categorisation. Whereas this might have merit within an academic setting where a certain rigour of categorisation is appropriate, in non-scholarly discourse it is a bit like suggesting abandoning the term "Christianity" itself. The very idea seems preposterous. Indeed, the diversity in Gnosticism is perhaps no greater than the diversity in Christianity. They may have a, more or less, similar theology, but what the Evangelicals are doing is radically different in some ways to what the Catholics are doing, yet no one is suggesting the abandonment of the term "Christianity".

Brakke (2010) provides what is, perhaps, the best model for understanding what is known as Gnosticism. Arguing that the notion of there being a single form of Christianity in antiquity was flawed, Brakke offers a new, "horse race" model of early Christian development. He suggests that, like horses in a race, there were a number of Christian groups in competition with one another, one of which came to dominate and consequently became the precursor to what we know today as Christianity. He claims that the various sects that are now considered to be Gnostic were simply horses in the race, along with a diverse range of other early forms of Christianity. The race just happened to be won by proto-Christianity. However, despite the utility Brakke's model may have, it rests on the assumption that the proto-Christianity horse was granted no special privilege, and that all horses in the race had a fair chance. It is very unlikely that was the case. In the horse race metaphor things are fairly black-and-white, the first horse past the post is the first horse past the post, and thus, the most fit-for-purpose, and rightfully declared the winner. In trying to understand Gnosticism's relationship with Christianity, an improvement on the horse race metaphor might involve an alternative model in which the winner, that is, proto-Christianity, was like a candidate chosen in an election, where the winning candidate is the one who may not necessarily be the most fit-for-purpose, but, at the time of the election at least, the voters believed would best serve their interests—or, more accurately, perhaps, were led to believe would best serve their interests.

For the purposes of this work, rather than the term "Gnosticism", which would include the history, the cultural milieu, the sects, the teachers, the credo, the rituals, and all the rest of it, the term "Gnostic" (adjective) is preferred. In this work, "Gnostic" is used to describe any one of a group of related spiritual worldviews, which are typically grounded in visionary experience, and which exhibit the following fundamental characteristics: (a) it is monistic: there exists a single, ineffable, transcendent ultimate divinity, out of which everything else comes into being; (b) its cosmogony involves a process of emanation of male-female syzygies out of the one transcendent source; (c) it is dualistic and draws a sharp distinction between a transcendent realm of light and the created world of matter; (d) the created world was not created by the ultimate divinity but was, instead, fashioned by a lesser, ignorant, occasionally evil, god and his subordinates; (e) creation resulted from some error or a disruption to the celestial order; (f) the creator god and his subordinates also created human beings, exiled them from their true home in the transcendent realm of light, and have imprisoned them in the world of matter; (g) each human being contains an innate spiritual essence which is one and the same as the essence of the ultimate divinity; (h) spiritual insight through direct inner experience is essential for salvation, and is therefore highly favoured over blind faith; (i) this salvific knowledge is imparted by an emissary from the transcendent realm, and (j) the goal of every Gnostic is to extract their divine essence from its imprisonment in the fallen world and return to its origin in the transcendent realm of light.

Stephan A. Hoeller (2002a), a scholar of both Gnosticism and Jungian studies, as well as a bishop of the Ecclesia Gnostica (a modern, revivalist Gnostic church), asserts that no spiritual tradition ceases to exist. Hoeller likens spiritual insight to the ripple in a pool caused by a fallen stone, emanating out for all eternity long after it has dropped out of human awareness. Gnosticism is no exception and, despite its apparent demise around the fourth century CE, it never really went away. However, it may have remained unknown in the public domain, and it would have been largely consigned to the dustbin of history, if it had not been for a few events which resulted in a resurgent interest in Gnosticism in our contemporary world.

First, there was the momentous discovery, in 1945, of the collection of Gnostic texts known as the Nag Hammadi Library, named after the small town in Upper Egypt close to where it was found. Its discovery was timely, if not synchronistic, just as one of the worst chapters in human history was coming to an end. The collection consists of fifty-three Gnostic texts in thirteen leather-bound papyrus codices which are considered to be the oldest known bound books in existence. Second, no matter how significant the discovery of the Nag Hammadi Library may have been, its contents, along with the spiritual philosophy of the Gnostics, would no doubt have remained of interest to only the most dedicated of scholars had it not been for the pioneering work of certain scholars who brought the Gnostics to a far wider audience, perhaps none more so than Professor Elaine Pagels, whose book, *The Gnostic Gospels*, published in 1979, was groundbreaking in this regard. According to pre-eminent author and scholar of Gnosticism, Richard Smoley (2006), Pagel's book, more than any other, including the Nag Hammadi Library itself, has introduced the general public to the ancient Gnostics. Third, in recent years there have been a number of Gnostic "revivalist" Churches—of which the aforementioned Ecclesia Gnostica is one—and movements, some of which reasonably assert their right to the epithet "Gnostic", and others for whom the claim is rather more tenuous. Fourth, as noted above, many people in the West are thirsty for an authentic spiritual life having become disaffected by Christianity's growing inability to be a worthy custodian of the West's spiritual heritage. In the absence, perhaps, of genuine religious containers, the void is partially filled by the prevalence of Gnostic themes in popular culture, exemplified by modern day movies such as *The Matrix, The Truman Show, Dark City, Pan's Labyrinth, 12 Monkeys, Vanilla Sky*, and *Pleasantville*, all of which, it has been claimed, contain Gnostic themes. Clearly, the motifs of the Gnostic tradition are re-emerging from the depths of the archetypal realms and are finding considerable resonance within contemporary Western society.

* * *

Personally, I first encountered the term "Gnosticism" when reading Jung's autobiography, *Memories, Dreams, Reflections* (1962), for the first time many years ago. I was immediately drawn to it in a way that went far beyond the mere piquing of curiosity. In fact, I experienced a much more profound, if subtle, resonance with the subject (i.e., Gnosticism), despite knowing absolutely nothing about it at that time. However, I would follow a rather circuitous route before taking a closer look at Gnosticism.

I once belonged to the group of Christian apostates who have sought spiritual nourishment beyond the institutions of Christianity. Consequently, I have done my share of browsing in what is often colloquially referred to as the spiritual supermarket. My first encounter with an alternative tradition was with Tibetan Buddhism. However, despite being fascinated by its spiritual philosophy, not to mention being seduced somewhat by its rich symbolism, I kept trying to reconcile the Buddhist teachings with Christian theology as I understood it. The two traditions seemed so very different—on the surface at least—such that either one (or both) had to be "wrong". Alternatively, they were both profoundly different expressions of a much deeper underlying truth. I reasoned that if I could reconcile these differences then I would be getting close to that truth, free of the idiosyncrasies of any one tradition. Perhaps in an attempt to resolve this conundrum, I was drawn to Paramahansa Yogananda's Self Realisation Fellowship, particularly due to his attempts to reconcile the teachings from *The Bible* with those from *The Bhagavad-Gita*. Around this time, I also encountered the works of the English Benedictine monk Fr Bede Griffiths who went to India to discover the other half of his soul. His writings had a major influence on me, in particular the *Marriage of East and West* (1982), and its efforts to point out the underlying unity of all traditions. A recognition for the need to reconcile opposites and seek deeper, underlying truths was instilled in me.

Yet, in my study of Eastern traditions something just did not fit, and I felt I could not fully belong in any of them. A religious tradition does not come into existence in a vacuum, but does so in a cultural context within which it is inextricably intertwined. Therefore, in order to get to the heart of a tradition, one must be able to differentiate between what belongs to the essence of the tradition, and what belongs to the cultural. Then there is the additional challenge of language. When a sacred text (or any other text) is translated from one language to another, something is always lost in translation, and the greater the difference between the source and target languages, the more that gets lost. Many words in English have their origin in either Latin or Greek and so it stands to reason that a text written in Greek, for example, will lose far less in translation when translated into English than a text translated from, for example, Sanskrit to English. Indeed, some concepts in Eastern traditions—and it must be remembered, we are dealing with concepts which are often ineffable—simply have no useful translation in English and are, therefore, often left untranslated in English versions. Thus, an English-speaking reader of an Eastern text translated into English generally needs some knowledge of Sanskrit (or Tibetan, etc.) before even beginning to grapple with the meaning of the text. Furthermore, there is always the sensitive, often thorny issue of the potential for cultural appropriation when one adopts a tradition from another culture.

For these reasons, no matter how much I appreciated and benefited from my encounters with Eastern traditions, I always felt that there was something missing for me. They seemed to lack, both literally and metaphorically, what I can only describe as soul. As a proponent of the Western Mystery Tradition has said, the rose of the West should not seek to bloom like the lotus of the East. This resonates strongly with me. Like a magnet, the teachings of the West kept pulling me back.

My attempts to reconcile my Christian background with a study of Eastern traditions reminds me of the parable of the blind men and the elephant, thought to originate in Theravadan Buddhism, and which later made its way into the Sufi tradition. One variant of the story teaches that three blind men approached an elephant, an animal with which they were unfamiliar. Without sight, they sought to know the animal through touch. One approached from the side and touched its leg, another from the front and felt its tusk, and the third, from the other side, touched its ear. When they compared their experiences, they soon discovered the discrepancies in their accounts. The man who had felt the leg described it as some kind of pillar, both rough on the surface yet yielded slightly under pressure. The man who had touched the tusk disagreed and described the elephant as a post, hard and smooth rather than soft and rough. The third man disputed the claims of the other two, describing the elephant as broad and rough like a piece of leather. Each was partially right based on their limited subjective experience yet none of them could fully comprehend the elephant. In other words, the subjective experience of each was true to some extent but, individually, they failed to grasp the objective truth (if there is such a thing). However, if they had realised the situation and pooled their knowledge they could have approached a more complete understanding of the elephant. Like myths and dreams, there is more than one way to interpret this teaching story. On the one hand, it speaks of the limitations of individual perception. Seen differently, each blind man represents the approach taken by different spiritual traditions in their attempts to comprehend the ineffable mysteries of the divine.

At the risk of mixing metaphors, a similar message can be found in the teachings of Zen master Basho who likened the various religions to different fingers pointing at the moon. As with the blind men, each finger provides only a partial truth. The inherent warning is that if we focus on the finger, we fail to grasp the moon. The role of the finger is simply to point beyond itself to the moon. In the same way that a GPS needs a clear line of sight to at least four satellites in order to determine an accurate geospatial location, perhaps we need a few fingers (i.e., differing spiritual perspectives) to accurately locate the "moon". If there is only one finger, and it is even slightly off in its alignment to the moon, then it will miss the moon. Similarly, if there are only two fingers pointing, and they are not pointing directly at the moon, then their point of intersection will not be at the moon. However, if there are three (or more) fingers, then their intersection will form a triangle (or polygon) and, even if the three fingers are all slightly off, there remains a good chance that the triangle of intersection will be the locus in which the moon is located. In other words, a variety of different perspectives can gives us a better, more rounded understanding of the object of our perception.

On the other hand, there can be too much of a good thing and there is an inherent risk in the overwhelming array of options presented by the spiritual supermarket. For Westerners that look beyond their native tradition for spiritual nourishment there is a veritable smorgasbord of wisdom traditions and teachers and practices to suit any taste. One is simply spoiled for choice and the inevitable cherry-picking can lead to an over-indulgence in spiritual chocolate cake, so to speak, while the spiritual broccoli goes untouched.

In *The Four Quartets*, the poet T. S. Eliot (1943) states that the end of our explorations leads us back to where we started, but having gained the ability to know, and understand, the place for the first time. For me, the end of my exploration of other traditions led me back to where I started, to my Christian roots in the broader sense, albeit in the form of Gnosticism. Decades of peregrination in the spiritual wilderness has not brought me to the Promised Land, but I at least feel that the Gnostics, both ancient and modern, have provided me with a map.

I will always be grateful for Eastern traditions and the insights those fingers at the moon have given me. The richness and texture they have provided to my spiritual understanding is inestimable. However, I am a Christian at heart—albeit a heretical one—with a Western soul and mind-set. Adapting a well-known adage; you can take the boy out of Christianity, but you cannot take Christianity—in some form—out of the boy. There might be one Truth, but there can be numerous expressions of that Truth. It has been said that there are many wells, but only one aquifer. For me, currently, it is the Gnostic Christian "well" from which I draw water.

Let me be absolutely clear here: in no way am I suggesting that Western traditions are in any way superior to Eastern traditions. I am simply stating that, for me, as a Westerner, Western traditions are, practically, linguistically, conceptually, and philosophically more accessible to me. There are many paths leading up the mountain. Why walk round to the other side of the mountain to take an alternative path? Why not take the path in front of me?

* * *

This book is not another work on Gnosticism which traces its history and attempts to detail the various Gnostic schools of antiquity, the teachers, the doctrines, and the practices and so on. That ground has been covered adequately by others. Rather, this book has two aims. The first is to present a comparison of the unique Gnostic (or "Gnostic-esque") worldviews of two figures who have done more than most to keep alive, indeed vivify, into the modern era what Smoley (2006) terms the Gnostic legacy. These modern day "Gnostics" (and here I use the term very loosely) are the Swiss psychologist, Carl G. Jung (1875–1961), and the American science-fiction writer, Philip K. Dick (1928–1982). (In this work, Dick will henceforth be referred to as "PKD", as he customarily is, with some affection it would seem, among his fan base.) Given the relatively recent publication of both Jung's and PKD's personal journals, *The Red Book* (Jung, 2009), and *The Exegesis of Philip K. Dick* (Dick, 2011), respectively, it seems timely to make this comparison. Both Jung and PKD had profoundly different approaches in arriving at their Gnostic visions. One was a depth (or transpersonal) psychologist whose unique insights and approach to psychology forced him to explore the depths of the unconscious in a way that inevitably led him to touch frequently on what might be considered metaphysical or spiritual matters. The other was an author of science fiction. Yet, as this book hopes to demonstrate, there are some striking parallels between their visions, all the more notable given their divergent starting points. However, whereas this book may ostensibly be about the Gnostic views of Jung and PKD, it is really an attempt to reframe Gnostic metaphysics in the light of their considerable contributions to the topic.

The book's second aim is to explore Gnostic spiritual philosophy in the light of these modern thinkers with the intention of presenting the ancient Gnostic myth in the language of modernity. Jung (1962) believed that a myth that remained static and did not evolve was, in effect, a dead myth; only a living myth can provide people with much-needed psycho-spiritual succour. In a not too dissimilar vein, PKD, commenting on a well-known Hermetic aphorism, "as above, so below", claimed that its author was trying to describe the universe as a hologram but lacked the terminology that we are familiar with today (Dick, 2001, pp. 257–258), and with which we can better describe and understand our world and our place in it. With these two ideas in mind, it is my hope to give the Gnostic tradition a modern "makeover" in the hope of not only making it more accessible to a contemporary audience, but also making a contribution to the continuation of the re-emergence of the Gnostic spirit, lest its renascent flame flickers briefly, sputters, and becomes extinguished once more.

* * *

One of PKD's later works, *VALIS* (2001), is a semi-autobiographical novel in which many of his favourite themes appear to have matured, and in which he presents his Gnostic vision. In a speech given at a conference at Metz in France in 1977, as he was writing *VALIS*, he describes how he appears as two different characters in the novel representing his ego and alter ego with two contrasting personalities: one a government researcher with a scientific bent, the other an unscientific person who is having unusual experiences which he does not understand and for which he has no theory (Dick, 1977). According to Dick, both approaches are required for the truth. Elsewhere, in his novel, *The Divine Invasion* (2008), he states, albeit referring to one of the characters in the novel, that he has two minds, one on the surface, and the other in the depths. In other words, one conscious, the other unconscious. Similarly, in *Memories, Dreams, Reflections* (1962), Jung refers to his No. 1 and No. 2 personalities, precursors to his ego and Self postulates, again, one conscious, the other largely unconscious. The need to reconcile the ego and the Self, or conscious and unconscious, in a way that listens to both perspectives, would become a hallmark of Jungian psychology. Therefore, in keeping with this theme, this work adopts a dual approach: a conscious researched—although not scientific—component, combined with an experiential component resulting from an engagement with the unconscious.

Given my background in transpersonal psychology, it is inevitable that this work is written from the perspective of that discipline. What is transpersonal psychology? Definitions are many and varied. As an academic discipline, transpersonal psychology explores the dimensions of human experience that extend beyond the personality and the generally very limited sense of personal identity, and it attempts to do so in a way that is grounded in a scientific or academic framework. Given its attempt to chart the full range of human existence, its field encompasses far more than psychology and a useful metaphor for it is that it attempts to bridge the domains of psychology and spirituality. In practice, transpersonal psychology typically seeks to create a synthesis of the theories and practices of a number of Western psychologies with the theories and practices of some of the world's wisdom traditions—notably those of the East, and those generally referred to as shamanic.

Transpersonal psychology challenges the privileged epistemological hegemony enjoyed by the traditional research methods (e.g., the scientific method) and what would normally be the accepted approach for a work such as this, that is, conventional "bookish" research. It argues that the normally accepted approaches to research are not the only ways of acquiring knowledge on a given subject and are, by no means, the best. For example, Hart, Nelson, and Puhakka (2000) argue that the "truths" of modern science, as well as religion, can no longer be seen as absolute truth, but must be taken as being relative to their context, be it the context of language, culture, epistemic assumptions, and so on. They claim that epistemological methods of both the sciences and the humanities have been "greatly humbled by [their] self-acknowledged limits" (p. 1), and that there is a growing recognition—one might add, a very slow and rather reluctant acceptance—of alternative ways of knowing. They advocate for an open and evolving approach to epistemology, which embraces multiple perspectives, and complements traditional methods with alternative approaches, and includes multiple disciplines, for example analysis and personal narrative.

The research for this work was premised on the notion that a single, definitive interpretation of a text is a fallacy. Interpretation is always a function of the interpreter and everything he, or she, brings to the work. Consequently, some degree of subjectivity—often quite pronounced—is inherent in any work. This book is no exception. Its unavoidable subjectivity is acknowledged. Indeed, it is welcomed, otherwise this work would be dry rational analysis, and nothing more than a report. The approach taken in researching this book assumed that understanding does not come from interpretation (or cognition) alone, rather it proceeds from a more holistic all-of-being engagement with the text in which intuition, the imagination, and felt sense are honoured alongside intellectual analysis. Meaning was allowed to emerge through heartfelt participation. Its method is one of entering into a dialogue with the text being researched, listening to it, and allowing it to communicate its message. The intent was to let the Gnostics speak to us once more through this work. Although this work has been researched as described, it is not intended as a scholarly work and, in an attempt to make it more reader-friendly, references have been kept to a minimum.

The primary resources for this work are Jung's *The Red Book*, PKD's *Exegesis*, and the Gnostic texts of the Nag Hammadi Library. Frequent references to canonical Christian scripture have also been made. Gnostic spiritual philosophy coincides with much of the essence of the early proto-Christianity prior to the latter's hijacking by Constantine et al., and its subsequent institutionalisation into a means of mass mind control—PKD suggests that the Church, as an institution, is "devoted to the betterment of a few and the exploitation of the many" (2008, p. 217). Nevertheless, a Gnostic can fruitfully learn from traditional Christian scripture. Paraphrasing the quasi-Gnostic poet William Blake (1757–1827), both Christians and Gnostics read the Bible day and night, but where one reads black, the other reads white. Another important resource, and inspiration, for this work is the motion picture *The Matrix* (Silver, 1999). Although it has drawn on multiple influences, not only Gnostic, *The Matrix* must surely be considered a modern-day Gnostic myth. It would be remiss of any work attempting to reframe the Gnostic myth in the language of modernity not to acknowledge it.

Transpersonal psychology also has a very strong focus on the experiential, and its empirical research methods need to include inner experiences which are crucial to the meaningful exploration of not only the psyche, but particularly metaphysical or spiritual realms. Therefore, this work complements the external knowing through the research approach (described above) with an inner experiential knowing through the practice of dream work.

Dream work was absolutely crucial to Jung, both personally and professionally. Along with its counterpart *active imagination* (which will be discussed in a subsequent chapter), dream work is the *sine qua non* of the application of Jung's psychology. Similarly, in his *Exegesis*, PKD (2011) claimed that the explorations contained therein came to him in "hundreds of dreams" (loc. 789). He also stated that he himself did not write his novels but that they come from within, from some other part of himself, and that they often contained his dreams (loc. 565). It is therefore fitting that this book, honouring the work of Jung and PKD, adopts dream work as its experiential approach. Once again the subjectivity in this approach is acknowledged, and, consistent with the major theme of this book, the reconciliation of opposites, a balance between objectivity, through research, and subjectivity, through dream work, has been sought.

The unconscious communicates in images. Therefore, it seems reasonable to suggest that any work that involves an exploration of the psyche, and attempts to dip its toe in the ripples that emanate from the ineffable depths of the unconscious—not to mention metaphysical realms—needs, in some way, to pay homage to symbols. During her adventures in Wonderland, Alice ponders what the use of a book without pictures is, and, with this in mind, this book contains a number of figures intended to help illustrate the points being discussed.

Finally, this work is in some ways a continuation of my previous book, *White Bird, Black Serpent, Red Book* (Douglas, 2016), insofar as it includes a further exploration of Jung's Gnostic vision. However, the present work is intended to be a standalone work and, as such, out of necessity, it has to reiterate some of the ground covered in my earlier work. I have endeavoured to keep this to a minimum.

* * *

It is my hope that this book will be of interest to not only those for whom the Gnostic worldview—particularly that of Jung and PKD—has a specific appeal, but also those Westerners (and others) who, having turned away from the orthodox religious tradition of their birth and, rather than looking to the East, have sought spiritual nourishment in the Gnostic tributary of the great underground river of the Western Mystery Tradition.

CHAPTER TWO

The living and the dead

The psychologist, Carl Gustav Jung, was born on July 26, 1875, at Kesswil on Lake Constance in Switzerland. Initially a follower and heir-apparent, indeed the crown prince, of Freud's emerging discipline of depth psychology, Jung would later break from Freud and develop his own form of depth psychology, which he termed analytical psychology in distinction to Freudian psychoanalysis. His greatest contributions to the field of psychology include the concept of the archetypes and the collective unconscious, of which the best known archetypes are the ego, the shadow, the anima/animus, and the Self; the psychological complex; and the psychological types, thinking, feeling, intuition, and sensation, along with the closely related psychological attitudes of introversion and extraversion. However, the cornerstone to his psychology is the process of individuation which he saw as central to human psycho-spiritual development and which attempted to reconcile and integrate all psychological opposites, principal among them being the ego/Self and conscious/unconscious. He died on June 6, 1961, at Küsnacht on the shores of Lake Zurich, aged eighty-five years.

* * *

Smoley (2006) notes the "tremendous contribution" (p. 163) Jung made in keeping the Gnostic flame burning and he credits Jung as "probably the single most powerful force in bringing [the Gnostic heritage] back to mass consciousness" (p. 159). A considerable achievement, no doubt, and even more remarkable when one remembers that Jung did so with only a paucity of Gnostic texts at his disposal—the cache of Gnostic texts known as the Nag Hammadi Library was not discovered until 1945, decades after Jung had completed his study of the Gnostics. Jung did, however, make a significant study of the Gnostic texts that were available to him, beginning as early as 1912, perhaps peaking around 1916—a year that proved to be crucial—and ending sometime around 1926. Jung's original Gnostic vision is articulated in a short text titled, *The Seven Sermons to the Dead*. The writing of the *Seven Sermons* was precipitated by a paranormal experience in which Jung felt his house was haunted by the spirits of dead people who announced to Jung that they had returned from Jerusalem without having found what they were looking for.

The Red Book, to which Jung initially gave the Latin title, *Liber Novus* (The New Book), is the published form of Jung's personal journal in which he studiously documents his enormously challenging encounters, over a two-and-a-half year period, with his inner psychological processes, and which he referred to as his confrontation with the unconscious (1962). The articulation of these encounters, as they appear in *The Red Book*, results from a technique Jung developed for working with the unconscious content that he was confronted with at that time. This technique involved giving a voice to suppressed and unknown aspects of the personality which are generally shunned or ignored. He called this technique *active imagination*.

Jung was a firm believer in the self-regulating nature of the psyche, indeed he considered it to be a basic law of psychic functioning. In the same way that many systems within the human body strive to maintain physiological homeostasis, he believed that the psyche attempts to maintain its own equilibrium in which any position taken consciously will elicit a corresponding counter-position in the unconscious. In a psychological restatement of Newton's third law of motion, Jung thought that for every force exerted by the conscious mind there will be an equal and opposite force exerted unconsciously. Furthermore, he felt that one of life's eternal conundrums was how does one come to terms with the unconscious, which, when reframed in terms of the theory of the self-regulating psyche, becomes, how does one reconcile the opposition between the conscious position and its corresponding unconscious counter-position? It was the urgent need to address the confusing and bewildering phantasmagoria of unconscious images, that threatened to overwhelm him during his confrontation with the unconscious, that compelled Jung to take up this challenge in earnest, and the means he developed for doing so was the technique of active imagination.

The process of active imagination involves giving some kind of expression to unconscious content (e.g., a dream image)—be it in the form of inner visualisation, artwork, writing, or dance—and then personifying that expression in some way, as if it were an autonomous being somehow separate from oneself, before entering into a dialectical exchange with that "other". The first step in the process of active imagination is to elicit the unconscious counter-position in the form of an image. Some might choose to make this image more concrete by drawing or painting it, turning it into a sculpture, writing it down, setting it to music in some way, or expressing its essence in dance or some other active or embodied form. For many, this might facilitate and enhance the experience of the image. Once the unconscious material has been obtained the next task is to hold a fixed image of it in the mind's eye with unwavering attention. This concentrated attention will, more often than not, animate the image and cause it to transform. It is important, at this point, to let the image unfold naturally, with as little interference as possible from the conscious mind which has the propensity to attempt to direct the process and thus run the risk of scuppering the enterprise. The changes to the fantasy images should be diligently noted because, according to Jung, they indicate the unconscious psychic processes which consist of images of conscious memories. In this way the dialectic of the opposites of conscious and unconscious has begun in the same way that a waterfall connects above and below (Jung, 1955–56). It is now that a reconciling dialogue of mutual respect and reciprocity can ensue between the conscious mind and the images of the unconscious. Crucial to the success of this method is that both the conscious and unconscious attitudes must be given their due in a peer-to-peer encounter that honours not only the equal rights of both participants (conscious and unconscious), but also seeks to balance the creative expression of the unconscious images with the need for conscious understanding.

Once the unconscious attitude has been given expression, and there has been a concerted attempt to understand its meaning, one comes to the most important part of the process which sees the tone of the endeavour shift from one of dialectical engagement to one of evaluation. Here it is imperative that one determines how one will relate to the unconscious content in a way that will allow the reconciliation of the differing conscious and unconscious positions, and, consequently, an integration of the unconscious material. Jung claimed that a failure to take this vital step left the practitioner of active imagination looking like Parsifal who, unaware of his participation in the process, failed to ask the vital question. Participation, rather than mere observation, is essential, hence the "active" in active imagination. If this step of evaluation and integration is accomplished, it can lead to the avowed purpose of active imagination, which is to integrate unconscious content with the conscious position, assimilate its (i.e., the unconscious) compensatory content, resulting in a holistic understanding that honours both positions, conscious and unconscious (ibid.).

Jung first articulated the process of active imagination in his essay "The Transcendent Function," written in 1916, the same year in which he recorded the last of his fantasies contained in *The Red Book* (although it would be some years before Jung transcribed these fantasies from his notebooks into what would ultimately come to be published as *The Red Book*). Subsequently, the integration of the conscious attitude with the unconscious counter-position, either through active imagination or dream work, would become central to analytical psychology to the extent that if Jung's entire psychology could be summed up in a single phrase it would be: the reconciliation and integration of the opposites. As will be explored below, the theme of the opposites, as it appears in the metaphysical concept of dualism, will prove to be central to the metaphysics of the Gnostic tradition.

Jung compiled *The Red Book* over a sixteen year period beginning in 1914 and ending in 1930. It contains Jung's visionary experiences from November 1913 to June 1916 which he had originally recorded in a series of notebooks before he began the endeavour of meticulously transcribing them into what we know today as *The Red Book*. Clearly, it was a work of enormous importance to him. However, it tails off abruptly in mid-sentence, and was therefore never completed, when his attention was directed towards projects which he presumably felt were of even more importance. Sweeping in scope, *The Red Book* is a multifarious panoply of Jung's repeated excursions into the realm of the unconscious. Above all else, however, it is one man's psychological quest for his lost soul which ultimately led him to the formulation of a new God-image framed, amongst other things, in a Gnostic psycho-cosmology. There are three parts to *The Red Book* and it is the final part, titled *Scrutinies*, which contains the *Seven Sermons*. It would appear that the *Seven Sermons* is a sublimation of the raw material of Jung's experiences of active imagination contained in the first two parts and this has resulted in Jung's unique Gnostic vision.

The *Seven Sermons* might also be considered as an epilogue to Jung's coming to terms with his break with Freud. Around 1913 Jung's close personal and professional relationship with Freud came to an end due to professional differences of opinion. It may not have been the most acrimonious parting of the ways, but it could hardly be described as amicable, even though Jung maintained a healthy respect for Freud—professionally, at least—for the rest of his life. Nevertheless, the split had a profoundly negative impact on Jung and it precipitated a period of enormous psychological challenge for him which he came to refer to as his confrontation with the unconscious. Emerging from this turbulent episode, Jung felt compelled to ground his experience in something concrete and, driven by this compulsion, he completed the *Seven Sermons* over the course of three evenings. The *Seven Sermons* is the only part of *The Red Book* that Jung allowed to be published (privately) during his lifetime. This initial publication bore the subtitle, *The seven instructions to the dead. Written by Basilides in Alexandria, where the East touches the West*, revealing not only its Gnostic inspiration, but, just as important, its central theme of the meeting of opposites. Towards the end of his life Jung would write, in *Memories, Dreams, Reflections* (1962), that the ideas presented in the *Seven Sermons* were precursors to all of his major contributions to depth psychology. As I argued in my first book, Jung's Gnostic vision was an inchoate form of analytical psychology (Douglas, 2016).

Despite holding a personal and professional interest in Gnosticism that remained with him throughout his life, Jung strenuously denied that he should be considered a Gnostic himself. He claimed, instead, to be a physician, whose psychology was grounded in empiricism, rather than being a philosopher, or mystic, or one given to metaphysical speculation. He repudiated the designation of his psychology as Gnostic as nothing more than the invention of his critics. Perhaps Jung's most adamant retort to such accusations (i.e., that he was a Gnostic) can be found in a letter, dated June 29, 1960, the year before he died (but not published until 1973), in which he responds to criticisms made by one of his principal theological critics, the Jewish philosopher, Martin Buber (1878–1965). In the letter, addressed to a certain Mr Smith, Jung denies that he makes any claims about the transcendental *per se* beyond what can be observed to occur in the psyche in relation to those things that might be considered transcendental or transpersonal. As such, he asserts a purely empirical approach that addresses psychic phenomena rather than anything metaphysical. Jung's view is that if the psyche posits the existence of God then his professional curiosity—duty, per-haps—compels him to examine the fact of such a psychic utterance, irrespective of the truth or otherwise of God's existence. Jung counters Buber's claim that he (Jung) is a Gnostic by noting that what Buber mis-interprets as Jung's so-called Gnosticism is, in fact, psychiatric observa-tion, a subject which Jung feels Buber knows nothing about. Jung goes on to suggest that Buber has based his misunderstanding of Jung's posi-tion on the *Seven Sermons*, which, in the letter to Smith, Jung attempts to downplay by describing it as a privately printed poem in the style of the Gnostics that he had intended only for a friend's birthday celebra-tion nearly half a century earlier (when Jung was forty-one). He claims it is nothing more than a poetic paraphrase of the psychology of the unconscious. The tone of the letter betrays the marked degree of irrita-tion with which it was clearly written, with Jung going to some length to explain that he investigates the phenomenon and observable fact of God as an autonomous complex in the psyche rather than God in itself. He proceeds to rail against theologians, such as Buber, who display such a marked degree of prejudice against science that it hinders them from understanding his empirical perspective. Jung concludes the letter by dismissing Buber's criticisms as coming from someone who is incom-petent in such matters, and who fails to understand the field, namely depth psychology, to which Jung has devoted his lifetime studying. Nice try Carl! That may have been the stance of Jung's public, professional persona, and it may even have convinced some people and allowed him to dodge the "Gnostic" epithet from time to time, but the man doth protest too much methinks. Jung's private metaphysical worldview was somewhat different entirely, and irrespective of his repeated deni-als, that worldview was decidedly Gnostic in orientation.

Nevertheless, despite the undeniable influence Gnosticism had on Jung and his psychology, can Jung be considered as a Gnostic? At the risk of sounding like a fence-sitter, rather than responding with a simple (or simplistic) "yes" or "no", it might be more appropriate—in a way that honours a man's life's work devoted to the tension of the opposites—to allow space for the ambiguity of an unanswered question. What is in no doubt, however, is that throughout his lifetime, Jung had a profound fascination with Gnosticism, made a "serious" study of the Gnostic texts that were extant during his time, and espoused a metaphysics— the *Seven Sermons*—which is unequivocally Gnostic, and which he attributes to Basilides, one of greatest Gnostic teachers of antiquity.

* * *

Philip Kindred Dick, born on December 16, 1928 in Chicago, USA, was a prolific, award-winning writer of science fiction. He authored forty-four published novels and around 120 short stories in that genre, and is best known for a number of his works which have been adapted for the big screen: *Blade Runner* (released in 1982, based on *Do Androids Dream of Electric Sheep?*), *Total Recall* (1990—and remade in 2012—based on the short story *We Can Remember It For You Wholesale*), *Minority Report* (2002, based on a short story of the same name), *Paycheck* (2003, based on a short story of the same name), *A Scanner Darkly* (2006, based on a novel of the same name), and *The Adjustment Bureau* (2011, based on the short story *Adjustment Team*). Although he was initially raised as a Quaker, PKD, like Jung, was a Christian, in PKD's case an Episcopalian, who, despite acknowledging the Gnostic character of his metaphysics, never disavowed his Christianity (Peake, 2013). PKD had a twin sister who died shortly after birth. This had a profound effect on PKD and would later be instrumental in shaping his Gnostic worldview. PKD died on March 2, 1982, aged fifty-three, following a stroke that had occurred two weeks earlier. His ashes were interred next to his twin sister whose tombstone had already been inscribed with PKD's name, along with her own, when she had died many years earlier (ibid.). In death, he was finally reunited with the twin he had sought so hard to be reconciled with in life.

* * *

Smoley (2006) asserts that, despite the fact that PKD had been a university dropout with little formal education, he had a better understanding of Gnosticism than anyone else in recent times, and that there were few, if any, in any time period, who had grasped the Gnostic tradition "so viscerally and expressed it [so] well" (p. 182). Whereas the experience that precipitated Jung's Gnostic vision, articulated in the *Seven Sermons*, was an encounter with the "dead", the experience that prompted PKD to embark on a quest that led to the formulation in his own Gnostic vision was, in contrast to Jung's experience, an encounter with the "living", namely, the entity PKD was later to term the Vast Active *Living* Intelligence System (or, VALIS, for short).

In much the same way that Jung's haunted house episode precipitated his writing of the *Seven Sermons*, PKD also experienced some kind of paranormal activity in his house just prior to the event that triggered the exploration—documented in his *Exegesis* (see below)—during which he formulated his Gnostic vision. In his semi-autobiographical novel, *VALIS*, he claims that during February 1974, his apartment had been saturated with high levels of radiation which resulted in an "aurora that sizzled … as if it were sentient and alive" (2001, p. 117). On the 20th of that month, he had an impacted wisdom tooth (in another account he claims it was two teeth) removed under anaesthetic. Later that day, after he had returned home, he was experiencing considerable pain and arranged for a local pharmacy to deliver some pain medication. Despite bleeding from the mouth and feeling weak from the ordeal, he answered the door himself—rather than let his wife answer—when the pharmacy delivery person arrived with the medication. When he opened the door, he found himself face to face with a dark-haired young woman who was wearing a gleaming, golden necklace in the shape of a fish, a Christian symbol that he claims was much in vogue in California during the counterculture movement of the 1960s. PKD quickly forgot his pain and, largely ignoring the woman and the pain medication, became transfixed by the fish pendant. He managed to ask the woman the significance of the fish symbol and she replied that it was a sign used by the early Christians. On hearing this, and momentarily dazzled by what he perceived to be a beam of pink light reflecting off the pendant, PKD immediately experienced a flashback—which he would later recount as an *anamnesis*—in which he was, himself, an early Christian in the time of ancient Rome. He briefly remembered a "furtive, frightened life as a secret Christian hunted by the Roman authorities" (ibid., p. 122). The flashback disappeared as quickly as it came and PKD found himself back in California in 1974 taking the pain medication from the delivery person. According to PKD, with the pink beam came understanding and "acute knowledge" (2008, p. 194), in other words, gnosis. It seems somewhat ironic that it was the removal of a "wisdom" tooth that triggered PKD's Gnostic epiphany, but that is PKD, and gnosis, for you. Given the date of this vision, and subsequent visions he experienced in the following month (March 1974), PKD adopted the shorthand term "2-3-74" to denote the experience. Elsewhere, he described it as his theophany, and his experience of the pink light beaming at him from the fish pendant is immediately reminiscent of the Christian mystic Jacob Boehme (1575–1624) who, in 1600, had a profound, mystical experience, lasting no more than fifteen minutes, in which he was captivated by a beam of sunlight reflected in a pewter dish (Madden, 2008). In his brief vision, Boehme felt that he saw directly into the nature of reality which involved a panentheistic God-concept. PKD's experience would appear to have had a somewhat similar effect and PKD, like Jung and his encounter with the dead, would spend the rest of his life attempting to fathom its depth and explicate its meaning. In the same way that Jung had his watershed moment in 1916, PKD had his in 1974. PKD claimed that his 2-3-74 vision was tied to his "entire intellectual life" (2011, loc. 4636). In the same way that Jung's entire life's work was an elaboration of the *Seven Sermons*, PKD's entire life's work was an "outgrowth and expression" (ibid., loc. 4636) of his 2-3-74 experience in the form of his science fiction novels.

Whereas PKD's Gnostic vision is summarised in his *Tractates Cryptica Scriptura* (Latin for "Treatise of Concealed Scripture"), it is more fully articulated in *The Exegesis of Philip K. Dick* (ibid.). The *Exegesis* is to PKD what *The Red Book* is to Jung. In the same way that *The Red Book* was Jung's attempt to rediscover his lost soul, PKD felt he had gained his soul through the explorations documented in the *Exegesis* (ibid., loc. 4018).

Jung (1962) claimed that his final major work, *Mysterium Coniunctionis* (1955–56) was his magnum opus but, from the point of view of anyone with a more mystical or metaphysical interest in his work, and certainly from the point of view of his Gnostic vision, his real magnum opus was *The Red Book* (2009), and, in particular, the *Seven Sermons*. In a similar vein, PKD claimed that *VALIS* was his magnum opus when, in fact, insofar as he articulates both his unique Gnostic worldview and his life's work, it might be more fitting to consider his *Exegesis* to be his magnum opus.

At times, while reading the *Exegesis*, it feels inspired; at others times, it feels like the work of a man possessed. PKD himself describes it as the "furtive act of a deranged person" (2001, p. 23). On the one hand, it can appear like the work of someone who has succumbed to hubris, and, on the other hand, it can appear to be the product of someone in the grip of psychological inflation. In Jungian psychology, the *mana* personality is the term used to describe an inflated ego that has identified with an archetype in a way that can be experienced as an invasion from the collective unconscious. Perhaps PKD was writing from his mana personality; in the *Exegesis* he frequently refers to *VALIS* as intruding upon this world. Nevertheless, regardless of whatever had taken hold of him, the *Exegesis* is, throughout, permeated by a sincere attempt to understand and explain his 2-3-74 experience and its full implications.

Notwithstanding his lack of formal education, PKD had an extensive knowledge of various religions, wisdom traditions, and philosophies. Consequently, in addition to the Gnostic worldview, the *Exegesis* draws on many sources—Christianity, Taoism, Buddhism, Platonism, Neoplatonism, and Hermeticism, among others. It might, therefore, be argued that I have ignored these other influences and been very selective in only highlighting the features of PKD's vision that correspond to Gnostic ideas. This is so, and I defend it on the grounds that it is almost impossible to discern what his final position is on anything. PKD's writing in his *Exegesis* is often paradoxical, which is entirely appropriate given the ineffable nature of the mysteries it seeks to explore; however, at other times it is simply self-contradictory where he reworks various aspects of his vision. PKD admits that his "... mind worries and scurries, contradicts itself, comes to conclusions and then arbitrarily drops them; the exegesis does not build. There is no accumulative factor" (2011, loc. 12010). Therefore, any tentative conclusions he draws in the final pages of the *Exegesis* do not appear to be any more "final" than those offered in the opening pages. In fairness of PKD, he probably never intended for the *Exegesis* to be published, at one point dismissing it as "a three-feet-high stack of chicken scratchings of no use to anyone else" (loc. 8949). Consequently, the reader is left with a rather free rein to make of it what he will, and all that the present work attempts to do is to illustrate that much of his vision is very much in accord with the Gnostics. In one entry, he claims that what he describes as the "hermetic hylozoic cosmology" of the Italian philosopher, Giordano Bruno (1548–1600), is the context in which he can best understand his experience. As a result, he declares Bruno as his "main man" (loc. 8071). Elsewhere he suggests that, in what sounds like an act of subversion, he has undermined the philosophy on which Western capitalist society has been founded, and reverted back to "hermetic, Gnostic Neoplatonism" (loc. 8128). However, despite the significant influence of Bruno, and many others, in the formation of PKD's worldview, there can be no denying the considerable parallels between his worldview and that of the Gnostics, and that his metaphysics is unquestionably Gnostic at heart. He claims that his life's work was to "restore Gnostic gnosis to the world in a trashy form [i.e., his science fiction novels]" (loc. 8587), and that the work "presents an unvarying cosmological schema in accord with the suppressed (Gnostic) doctrines" (loc. 5891).

Like Jung, PKD was a reluctant Gnostic and somewhat loath to accept being characterised as such. He notes (1978) that he has been "accused" of being sympathetic to Gnostic ideas, an accusation which he tentatively accepts before noting drily that in the past he would have been burned at the stake for his heretical ideas. In his *Exegesis*, he claims that anyone who was acquainted with Gnosticism would consider him to be a Gnostic, to which he reacts: "I am not happy about this" (loc. 4370). Elsewhere, he claims that his explication of his vision is derived from revelation and "does not fit the model" (loc. 6831) he would rather believe in. Yet, despite any disquiet he may have experienced at the idea of his metaphysics being Gnostic, he reluctantly concedes that he is too far into Gnosticism "to back out" (loc. 5761), and, thus, he clearly, albeit grudgingly, accepts that his 2-3-74 vision is Gnostic. In his *Exegesis*, he declares that he has fulfilled his allotted task and its essence is the gnosis of the Gnostics (loc. 8248).

* * *

In summary, some striking parallels can be seen between the Gnostic works of both Jung and Dick (Figure 2). Both had a mystical experience triggered by what can only be described as paranormal activity. Both had Gnostic visions as a result of these experiences and which are articulated in relatively short texts, the *Seven Sermons*, and the *Tractates Cryptica Scriptura*. Both engaged with the unconscious, particularly through dreams, and claimed their visions were the result of revelation rather than ratiocination. Both spent the rest of their lives trying to understand and explain their Gnostic visions.

The remainder of this book will explore the correspondences between their respective visions in greater detail.

	Jung	*PKD*
Gnostic vision:	The *Seven Sermons to the Dead*	The *Tractates Cryptica Scriptura*
Gnostic vision precipitated by:	Paranormal activity: haunted house full of spirits, the "dead".	Paranormal activity: pink beam from VALIS, the "living".
Public opus:	*Mysterium Coniunctionis*	*VALIS*
Private opus:	*The Red Book*	*The Exegesis of Philip K. Dick*
Methods of insight:	1. Dreams 2. Active imagination	1. Dreams 2. Hypnogogic/ hypnopompic states of consciousness
Elaboration of Gnostic vision:	Jung's whole career after the *Seven Sermons* was an explication of ideas contained in it. Analytical psychology is founded on the *Seven Sermons*.	PKD spent the rest of his life trying to understand and explain his 2-3-74 experience.

Figure 2. Summary of the Gnostic works of Jung and PKD.

CHAPTER THREE

Ex nihilo, ex plenitudo

The All-Transcendent, utterly void of multiplicity, is Unity's Self, independent of all else … It is the great beginning, wholly and truly one. All life belongs to it.

—Plotinus

Both the first book of the Old Testament of the Christian Bible, as well as the most mystical of the canonical Gospels of the New Testament, *The Gospel of John*, begin their cosmogonies, quite logically it would seem, in the beginning: "In the beginning God created the heaven and the earth" (Genesis 1:1, King James Version [KJV]), and, "In the beginning was the Word, and the Word was with God, and the Word was God. The same was in the beginning with God" (John 1:1–2, KJV). On the other hand, Gnostic cosmogonies typically begin with an eternal realm *before* the beginning or, more accurately, outside of time altogether. For example, *The Secret Book of John* (a.k.a. *The Apocryphon of John*) of the Nag Nammadi Library teaches that the ineffable ultimate mystery, the One, is illimitable, unfathomable, immeasurable, invisible, unutterable, and unnameable, since nothing existed before it in order to limit it, fathom it, measure it, and so on. It is eternal since it is beyond time. Rather than being considered God, or a god, or even being likened to a god, the One should be thought of as being greater than a god, with nothing over it and nothing preceding it. Similarly, the text *Eugnostos the Blessed* teaches that the ultimate divinity should be addressed as Forefather rather than Father. The Father is the beginning of the universe but the Lord is the Forefather without a beginning (Meyer, 2007).

The Dominican theologian, and perhaps Christianity's greatest mystic, Meister Eckhart (1260–1327), proposed that, whereas theologians might argue, the mystics of the world spoke the same language. In the following description of the ineffable One, Eckhart is certainly speaking the same language as the Gnostic mystics:

> But the perfect reflection of the One is shining by itself in lonely silence, there safely pent as one and indivisible. The unity (of God) is un-necessitous, it has no need of speech, but subsists alone in unbroken silence. ... O unfathomable void, bottomless to creatures and to thine own self, in thy depth art thou exalted in thy impartible, imperishable actuality; in the height of thy essential power thou art so deep thou dost engulf thy simple ground which is there concealed from all that thou are not.
>
> (Meister Eckhart)

For the Gnostics, not only is the One beyond time, in other words, non-temporal, the One is also non-spatial. *The Teachings of Silvanus*

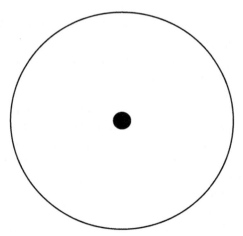

Figure 3. The Monad. The One.

informs us that it is incorrect to conceive of God as being in a place as this would localise God thus exalting the place over the one who exists there given that the container is deemed to be superior to that which is contained. Echoing the ancient Greek philosopher Empedocles (c. 490–c. 430 BCE)—who subscribed to a monist perspective and likened the nature of God to a circle of which the centre is everywhere and the circumference is nowhere (Figure 3)—*Silvanus* taught that the One was simultaneously in every place, but also in no place, insofar as the power of the One is everywhere but the essence of the One's divinity cannot be limited to any one place because nothing can contain it. For the ancient Gnostics, the One was a transcendent, ineffable mystery beyond both time and space.

* * *

There is no single Gnostic creation myth, although the creation myth in *The Secret Book of John* might be considered by some to be the de facto standard. Rather, Gnostic creation myths are varied and, more often than not, convoluted to a seemingly excessive degree. Often they tend to obfuscate rather than illuminate. Therefore, the simplified description presented here is a general synthesis, drawn from a number of creation myths in the Nag Hammadi Library. Hopefully, it highlights the salient features of Gnostic cosmogony without getting mired in the often unintelligible details.

Gnostic creation myths can typically be categorised as forms of monism. In other words, they conform to the metaphysical doctrine that conceives reality as a unified whole founded on a single, indivisible, and eternal entity known as the monad. In Gnostic cosmogony, the monad is considered to be wholly transcendent, ineffable, immaculate, incorruptible, and, from the point of view of the human mind, unknowable. It is completely alien to the created world (Figure 4). The various Gnostic schools referred to this monad differently. For example, the Sethians referred to it as the Great Invisible Spirit, whereas others, such as the followers of the Gnostic teacher Basilides, referred to it as the Pleroma. This ultimate divinity is better conceived of as non-being, rather than *a* being, as it is beyond being itself. It is a God-above-God, and more akin to the Godhead of Meister Eckhart's metaphysics, rather than God. It reposes in peace, outside of time in the unfathomable depths of silence.

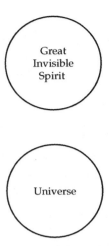

Figure 4. The Great Invisible Spirit and the universe. In Gnostic cosmology, the monad, the Great Invisible Spirit, is wholly transcendent and alien to the manifest universe.

In mainstream Christian theology, the doctrine of creation maintains that God, through an act of will, created the universe *ex nihilo* (out of nothing) and, as such, creator and creation are separate. In contrast, Gnostic cosmogony is emanationist in that it sees the universe as coming into being through a process of emanation out of the fullness (*ex plenitudo*) of the Great Invisible Spirit. The entire created realm, or universe, came into being from this primal unity through a process of successive emanations of male/female binary opposites with each pair, taken together, forming what is termed a *syzygy*. Out of the nothingness of the Great Invisible Spirit, came the fullness of the paired opposites. These emanated beings, or powers, are referred to by the Gnostics as *aeons*, and together they constitute the fullness of the Great Invisible Spirit in a way that is not unlike the way Jung's concept of the collective unconscious is comprised of the archetypes. The last of these aeons is Sophia, Holy Wisdom, who, in Christianised forms of Gnosticism, forms a syzygy with her consort, Jesus Christ. Contemporary Gnostic priest, Jordan Stratford (2007), likens this process of emanation to a stone dropped into a still body of water. The peak and trough of the waveform initiated by the first splash of the stone represented the primordial and eternal binary opposites, emptiness/ fullness, potential/actual, male/female, yin/yang, and so on. As each succeeding pair became further removed from the original perfection they became increasingly more material with the transition from the immaterial realm of light to the material realm resulting from an error, rooted in ignorance, which led to a disruption of the aeonic harmony in the Pleroma. This creation-as-error is a principal theme of Gnostic cosmogony. For example, *The Gospel of Philip* states emphatically that the world came into being through error. This error is typically attributed to Sophia who, feeling estranged from the primal unity, sought to emulate the Great Invisible Spirit. In an act of passion she attempted to emanate out of herself. However, she did so without the approval of the Spirit and without the consent of her consort, and the result was an imperfect and deformed bastard offspring called *Yaldabaoth* who is known as the *demiurge* (or "creator", derived from a Greek word that originally meant "craftsman" or "artisan"). The demiurge is described as the ignorant darkness, and in symbolism he is typically represented as having the head of a lion and the body of a snake, or a dragon, and eyes that flash lightning bolts (Figure 5).

Subsequently, the demiurge, in collusion with his underlings, the *archons*, created, through an act of ignorance, the material world, and then the first human. First, the demiurge attempted to fashion a world in the "indestructible pattern" of the first aeons of the Pleroma. However, he is a blind (ignorant) god and therefore cannot actually

Figure 5. A lion-faced deity thought to represent the demiurge.

see the indestructible realm, he can only perceive it dimly due to the power he received from his mother. Consequently, the created world is a counterfeit world fashioned by the counterfeit spirit of the demiurge and his archons. Once complete, the demiurge surveys his creation and declares to his archons that he is God, and, like the God of the Old Testament, he is a jealous God claiming there to be no other gods but him. Of course in stating this—as *The Secret Book of John* points out—he thereby admits that there must, indeed, be another God, otherwise of whom could he possibly be jealous? Second, the archons, under the direction of the demiurge, created the first human. However, the human they created was a psychic and material body only, and lacked the spirit of light to animate it. Having seen the work of the demiurge and his archons, Sophia now repented at what she had instigated and prayed for forgiveness. Answering her prayer, the Great Invisible Spirit outwitted the ignorant demiurge into blowing the spirit that the demiurge had received from his mother, Sophia, into the first human. As a result, the light left the demiurge and entered the first human bringing him to life. Realising that the first human contained the light that they lacked, the archons became jealous and cast him down into the lowest reaches of the material world where, according to the Gnostics, he remains a prisoner.

The Gnostic schools of antiquity flourished in the city of Alexandria in Egypt, and the Egyptian religion no doubt provided an inspiration, if not the direct source, for the Gnostic creation myths. The most ancient creation myth of the Egyptians is that of Atum (Ellis, 2012). First, there was nothing, and out of the nothingness, Atum came into being because becoming is his nature. Like the Great Invisible Spirit of the Gnostics, Atum is considered to be the absolute reality, and is described as immaculate, incorruptible, and so on. He is considered to be the God of the beginning and the end, and, as such, is outside of time. Everything emanated out of Atum, and, at the end of time, everything will return to Atum (ibid.). "I am Alpha and Omega, the beginning and the ending, saith the Lord" (Book of Revelation 1:8, KJV) immediately comes to mind. Atum begins creation by bringing forth twins. He sneezes out Shu, the god of dry wind, and spits out Tefnut, the goddess of moisture (ibid.), and the whole of creation proceeds from this first pair. (It sounds like we are nothing more than the by-product of some gooey stuff that flew out of God's nose.) Next come the goddess Nut, the water of Heaven, and her husband-brother Geb, the god of Earth. Thus, as for the Gnostics, creation proceeds as the emanation of male/female syzygies out of a primal nothingness.

The key principle of Gnostic cosmogony is not so much the idea of creation-as-error, but the idea that inherent in the process of the creation of the material world is a profound disruption to divine harmony. When Sophia decided to create on her own without the consent of her partner it resulted in a rupture to the balance of the primal syzygy, which, in turn, led to the birth of the demiurge, the archons, and the created world. If the primal syzygy had remained in perfect balance, unity would have persisted and the manifest universe could not possibly have come into being. This world *required* the harmonious balance to be disturbed and, as a result, disorder is not merely an unfortunate by-product of creation but, in the Gnostic tradition, one of the fundamental principles on which it is founded.

* * *

And what, Socrates, is the food of the soul? Surely, I said, knowledge [gnosis] is the food of the soul.

—Plato

Gnosis (derived from the Greek word *gnōsis* meaning "knowledge") refers to direct, unmediated, experience *of* the divine, as opposed to knowledge, in the sense of information—typically someone else's—*about* the divine. It is not unique to the Gnostic tradition. In one form or another, it is the *sine qua non* of all forms of mysticism; other traditions simply refer to it by other names. However, as the name suggests, it is indispensable to the Gnostic worldview, and its attainment considered essential to achieving salvation and the ultimate goal of Gnostic systems which is to return to the Pleroma. To have experienced gnosis would be to have had a mystical experience through which one has grown spiritually, and to have attained, or acquired, gnosis would be to have completed spiritual development, a state which is, more or less, the direct correlation of having attained enlightenment in Eastern systems. In other words, gnosis accrues incrementally through mystical experience, and one can be described as having attained full gnosis upon reaching complete spiritual awareness. As gnosis is seen as essential for humanity's salvation, then its corollary holds that—as is claimed, for example, in the *Authoritative Discourse* of the Nag Hammadi

Library—ignorance is the worst sin. Thus, the Gnostic tradition shares the view with Buddhism that enlightening wisdom is salvific, and ignorance, considered to be one of the three "poisons" in Buddhism, is antithetical to salvation. Similarly Jung believed that humanity's worst sin was unconsciousness and that knowledge of the truth of the human condition was essential for psycho-spiritual growth and ultimate salvation. So too did PKD realise the need for gnosis. Indeed, he claimed that the gnosis which the Gnostics sought was the only road to our salvation (2001, p. 265).

* * *

Like most Gnostic creation myths, Jung's Gnostic vision, articulated in the *Seven Sermons*, begins with nothingness. Paradoxically, this nothingness is also the fullness. The nothingness is, simultaneously, both empty and full. Like some of the ancient Gnostics before him, Jung referred to this nothingness/fullness as the Pleroma. Danish Nobel Prize-winning quantum physicist, Niels Bohr (1885–1962), is reputed to have stated that the opposite of a fact is a falsehood, whereas the opposite of one profound truth may be another profound truth. In a similar vein, it would appear that, whereas in the mundane, everyday world of so-called reality, paradox does not make any sense, in the ineffable realms paradox, according to the Gnostics—and possibly Bohr, if some kind of parallel can be drawn between the ineffable and the quantum realms—is a fundamental principle. Thus, in keeping with the paradoxical nature of the ineffable, the Pleroma is, simultaneously, both the fullness and the emptiness. (It is worth noting in passing that, such was the importance of duality as a fundamental law of reality to Bohr, that when a Danish knighthood was conferred on him, he designed his own coat of arms to include the Taoist yin-yang symbol (Rosenblum & Kuttner, 2012). As will be discussed below, duality, or the theme of the opposites, is the very crux of Gnostic metaphysics.)

The nothingness/fullness of Gnostic cosmology might be usefully described as mitigated *apophatic* theology. Apophatic theology is a theological stance that considers the ultimate divinity to be ineffable to such a degree that the only way we can speak of it is by way of negation. This is in contrast to *cataphatic* theology which attempts to define the divine in terms of what it is—an approach which the adherents of the apophatic perspective reject as they see it as an attempt to limit the illimitable. As noted above, *The Secret Book of John* alludes to the Great Invisible Spirit, rather than defining it, by describing it as illimitable, unfathomable, immeasurable, etcetera. Jung's Pleroma is apophatic in its nothingness yet, in containing the fullness within itself, its apophatism is mitigated. It has no qualities, yet it contains all qualities in a state of potential. Jung's Gnostic view of the Pleroma shows up in his "Psychological Commentary on 'The Tibetan Book of the Great Liberation'" (1954). Commenting on the Eastern concept of One Mind, which is a direct correlate of both the Pleroma and the collective unconscious, he states that it is without characteristics. It cannot be said to be created, or non-created, as these designations would be characteristics. Indeed, no assertions can be made about it at all since it is "indistinct, void of characteristics and, moreover, 'unknowable'" (p. 133).

However, there is one fundamental point of departure between Jung's concept of the Pleroma and the Great Invisible Spirit of the Gnostics. For the Gnostics, the ultimate divinity is completely alien and a wholly transcendent God-above-God; Jung's Pleroma is simultaneously, and paradoxically (again), fully transcendent yet fully immanent. Whereas Jung inherits the Gnostic view that the created world is estranged from its source in the ineffable realm, his concept of the Pleroma remains intimately related to the created world. In much the same way that light pervades the atmosphere, and electromagnetic radiation penetrates solid objects, Jung's Pleroma interpenetrates the created world. For the Gnostics, the Great Invisible Spirit is, in a spatio-temporal sense, distant from creation. For Jung, this spatio-temporal separation has been collapsed and the Pleroma pervades creation. This is in accord with the maybe not-quite-Gnostic *Gospel of Thomas* which teaches that splitting a piece of wood, or lifting up a stone, and there within can be found the divine. As such, in contrast to the monist cosmology of the ancient Gnostics, Jung's Gnostic vision is *panentheistic*. Panentheism (from the Greek *pan* "all", *en* "in", and *theos* "God" [i.e., "all in God"]), in distinction to *pantheism*, is the metaphysical doctrine that considers God to be greater than the universe, both containing it and interpenetrating it. God is simultaneously transcendent and immanent. Pantheism (from the Greek, meaning "all is God"), on the other hand, identifies God with the universe, in other words, the universe is God manifest, and God is the universe un-manifest (Figure 6).

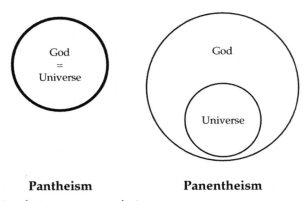

Pantheism   **Panentheism**

Figure 6. Pantheism vs. panentheism.

However, despite a general absence of panentheism in Gnostic scripture, there is at least a hint of it in *The Gospel of Philip* which suggests that, rather than the usual characterisations of the divine realm as "higher" and the created realm as "lower", it would be better to reframe these as "inner" and "outer". Drawing on the following passage from the canonical *Gospel of Matthew*, "When thou prayest, enter into thy closet, and when thou hast shut thy door, pray to thy Father which is in secret" (Matthew 6:6, KJV), *Philip* asserts that what is innermost is the fullness of the Pleroma and what is outermost is the darkness of the corrupt world. Jung's model of the Pleroma would fit more readily to the inner/outer model (minus the corruption) than the higher/lower model that characterises most of Gnostic thought. Jung's vision also shares the panentheism of the *Corpus Hermetica* which teaches that it would be incorrect to think that matter could exist apart from God. If it did, it would be nothing but a confused mass. Matter is inherently ordered and that order is of God. The energies that operate within matter are parts of God who is in all. In the Hermetic view, there is nothing that is not God.

For Jung, like the Hermeticists, if not the Gnostics, the Pleroma interpenetrates the material world and the distinction between the immaterial and the material is one of quality, or state, rather than a spatio-temporal separation.

Jung's Gnostic cosmogony also differs from that of the ancient Gnostics' in terms of process. Expanding on the concept of emanation of the binary pairs of opposites, Jung's account stresses the crucial importance of the differentiation of the opposites in the act of creation. For Jung, differentiation *is* creation, and without the differentiation of the opposites, there can be no creation. Without differentiation, the syzygies of the Pleroma remain inert and exist, insofar as they can be considered to exist at all, as potentials only. Through the process of differentiation, these original unified "pairs"—we cannot really call them pairs in their unified, undifferentiated state—are split into a dyad of complementary, yet polar, opposites, both of which are required to reconstitute the whole. Nothing can exist without the simultaneous existence of its complementary opposite. There is no hot without cold, no light without dark. In the Pleroma, prior to differentiation the opposites cancel one another out and are ineffective and not "real". Only once differentiated do they come into effect and become what we might consider as "real". Consequently, as created beings, the fundamental characteristic of human nature in Jung's Gnostic thinking is the differentiation of the opposites. This differentiation of the opposites would become the crucial factor and the hallmark of Jung's psychology.

Also lacking from Jung's Gnostic creation myth is the notion that the world came into being through error. Indeed, in sharp contrast, Jung's view was that the process of emanation/differentiation of the pairs of opposites was to be regarded, not as a mistake, but far more positively as the origin of life itself (McGuire & Shamdasani, 2012).

* * *

In the fashion of the Gnostic myths of antiquity, PKD's Gnostic cosmogony also begins with the monad, which he defines in his *Exegesis*, quite simply, as the "sentience in the cosmos which understands" (2011, loc. 7129). Out of this monad the opposites emerge. In the *Tractates Cryptica Scriptura* he writes, "One Mind there is; but under it two principles contend" (2001, p. 257). Sharing the paradoxical nature of Jung's Pleroma, PKD's ultimate reality, the One Mind, both is and is not. PKD describes a two source cosmogony that resulted from the One's desire to differentiate the "was-not from the was" (p. 266). Like Jung's Gnostic myth, differentiation is at the very heart of coming-into-beingness in PKD's gnosis. This desire to differentiate led to the formation of what he refers to as a "diploid sac" containing a pair of androgynous twins, spinning in opposite directions, symbolising the yin and yang of Taoism with the

One representing the Tao itself. Diploid (from Greek *diploos*, meaning double) is a biological term that refers to a cell containing two sets of chromosomes, typically one set from the mother and the other from the father. Thus, PKD's use of the term "diploid" highlights the primary syzygy fundamental to Gnostic cosmogony. Taoism had a profound influence on PKD's worldview (as it did on Jung's) and this influence is evident here. Strong parallels between PKD's cosmogony and the teachings of the *Tao Te Ching* are clear. For example,

> There was something undefined and complete, coming into existence before Heaven and Earth. How still it was and formless, standing alone, and undergoing no change, reaching everywhere … It may be regarded as the Mother of all things.
>
> (Chinese philosopher Lao-Tze)

Like the classic Gnostic myths, and in contrast to Jung, PKD's cosmogony also results from an error. The original plan of the One was for the androgynous twins to be birthed from the diploid sac simultaneously. However, in an act reminiscent of Sophia's desire to create on her own as found in *The Secret Book of John*, the anticlockwise twin, motivated by the desire for existence, emerged from the sac prematurely and defectively, somewhat akin to Sophia's bastard child, the demiurge. PKD refers to this premature twin as the dark, yin twin. The other, the yang twin, which PKD describes as wiser, only emerged at full term and was without defect. The result was that each twin was "a unitary entelechy, a single living organism" (2001, p. 266) consisting of both psyche and soma, but continuing to spin in opposite directions. However, the premature birth of the yin twin gave rise to a decaying condition which introduced "malefactors"—much like the demiurge and the archons—which, in turn, led to the origin of "entropy, undeserved suffering, chaos and death" (p. 266) and what PKD would refer to as the Black Iron Prison (see below). Elsewhere, consistent with the Gnostic view that the created world came into being as a result of a rupturing of the divine harmony of the aeonic syzygies, PKD (2008) asserts that the created world resulted from a rupturing of the Godhead. Due to a "primordial schism" (p. 158), part of the Godhead remained in the transcendent realm, and the other part became debased and fell to become the created world. Consequently, the "*Godhead [has] lost touch with a part of itself*" (p. 158, emphasis in original).

Following the emanation of the original twins, the next step was that the two became many through a process of dialectical interaction in which "[F]rom them as hyperuniverses they projected a hologram-like interface, which is the pluriform universe we creatures inhabit" (Dick, 2001, p. 266). Once established, the universe needs to be maintained by an equal intermingling of the original twins. Thus, for PKD, as for Jung, the universe remains in existence due to the interaction of the opposites. PKD's cosmogony is undoubtedly a unique variation on the theme, but it is unmistakably Gnostic at its core. It results in two realms (Figure 7), the upper, or yang, which he describes as sentient and volitional, and the lower, or yin, which he describes as "mechanical, driven by blind, efficient cause, deterministic and without intelligence, since it emanates from a dead source" (ibid., p. 269). Like the ancient Gnostics who believed we were trapped in an alien world, and estranged from the Pleroma, PKD believed that we are trapped in the lower realm.

A key feature of PKD's Gnostic cosmology is its *acosmic* panentheism. PKD defines panentheism as a metaphysical doctrine that states that God is simultaneously both transcendent and immanent, in other words, both beyond all, yet within all (2011, loc. 18161). Like Jung, PKD's Gnostic vision echoes *The Gospel of Thomas* in which the divine can be found when a piece of wood is split or when a stone is lifted up. PKD's panentheism led him to claim that God is as near at hand "as the trash in the gutter—God is the trash in the gutter, to speak more precisely" (1977). This notion immediately brings to mind Christ's birth in a stable among the animals. It is also reminiscent of the alchemical concept of lead being turned into gold or, rather more prosaically, the shit of daily life is the raw material for the transformation of the individual

Figure 7. The upper and lower realms in PKD's Gnostic vision.

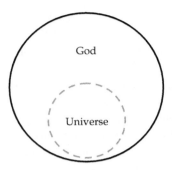

Figure 8. Acosmic panentheism.

soul. Acosmism, on the other hand, is a metaphysical or philosophical concept that denies any substantial reality to the universe. Instead, only the absolute has any reality and the universe is merely an illusion. Combined, with panentheism, acosmic panentheism posits an ultimate divine reality greater than, and encompassing, an unreal, or illusory, universe (Figure 8).

For PKD, God is greater than the world, or the universe, and only God is wholly real. However, God is enshrouded in an illusory "veil of appearance" (2011, loc. 4910) which PKD likens to a multifaceted sphere where each facet emits a coloured light, somewhat akin to the mirrored disco balls of yesteryear. According to PKD, acosmism is intrinsic to the gnosis of the Gnostics (loc. 9324).

* * *

The Gnostic cosmogonies of Jung and PKD share a number of significant correspondences; however, they differ in the detail, with perhaps the most fundamental difference between their respective visions being that for Jung the universe is real—at least, he does not appear to have questioned its fundamental existence—whereas for PKD, it is not real. This theme will be explored in greater detail in a later chapter.

CHAPTER FOUR

The darkness and the light

If yin and yang do not exist, the One (the Great Ultimate) cannot be revealed. If the One cannot be revealed then the function of the two forces will cease. Reality and unreality, motion and rest, integration and disintegration, and clearness and turbidity are two different substances. In the final analysis, however, they are one.
—Chinese philosopher, Chang Tsai, 1020–1077

The Gnostics are invariably categorised—often pejoratively—as being dualist, and this designation, minus the deprecation, is, by and large, correct. However, the Gnostic tradition is no more dualistic than Judaeo-Christianity which teaches that,

In the beginning God created the heaven and the earth.
And the earth was without form, and void; and darkness was upon the face of the deep. And the Spirit of God moved upon the face of the waters.
And God said, Let there be light: and there was light.
And God saw the light, that it was good: and God divided the light from the darkness.

41

And God called the light Day, and the darkness he called Night.
And the evening and the morning were the first day.
(Genesis 1:1–5, KJV)

Thus, dualism appears in the very first line of the Old Testament of the Christian Bible; Heaven and Earth, immediately followed by light and dark, day and night.

Perhaps some clarification on the use of the term "dualist" is warranted. The terms "dualist" and "dualism" are derived from the Latin word *duo*, meaning "two" and, at its simplest, dualism refers to the state in which something has been split into two equal parts, thus forming, in the strictest sense, a binary opposition—that is, a complementary pair with opposite natures—where each one of the pair can only be conceived in terms of its opposite, for example, hot and cold, light and dark, and so on. Furthermore, there are different types of dualism. In the branch of philosophy known as the Philosophy of Mind, in which the chief concern is the exploration of the non-physical mind and its relationship to the physical body and the rest of the physical world, dualism refers specifically to the mind-body dichotomy. A leading proponent of this philosophical stance was the French philosopher René Descartes (1596–1650) who famously declared, "cogito ergo sum" (I think, therefore I am). In theology, on the other hand, dualism generally refers to the notion that God and creation are fundamentally separate, whereas, in metaphysics, dualism tends to be seen ontologically in which the universe is thought to be founded on the principle of polar opposites such as light and dark, good and evil, or, in the Taoist tradition, yin and yang.

Ontological dualism is further divided into absolute (or radical) dualism and mitigated dualism. In absolute dualism there are two opposing principles which are each given equal status. Manichaeism—often linked to, but distinct from, Gnosticism—and Zoroastrianism are examples of absolute dualistic philosophies (although in the case of Zoroastrianism, the deck seems to be stacked in favour of the light principle as it is generally considered that it will, ultimately, win out over the principle of darkness—so perhaps not quite absolute after all). On the other hand, in mitigated dualism, there is an imbalance between the relative power and importance of the two principles with one seen as superior.

Gnostic cosmology is, primarily, a form of mitigated dualism, although it can also be considered to contain, secondarily, a form of

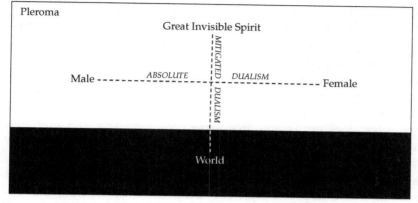

Figure 9. Mitigated and absolute dualism in Gnostic cosmology.

absolute dualism (Figure 9). First, in what might be considered a vertical axis, there is a mitigated dualism insofar as the Great Invisible Spirit is considered superior to, and set apart from, a corrupt world of darkness that imprisons humanity. Second, in what might be considered the corresponding horizontal axis, there is an absolute dualism in terms of the androgynous, male/female, aeonic pairs, or syzygies, which have emanated from the Pleroma and exist in binary opposition to one another (e.g., good and evil, light and dark, etc.).

Not only is dualism fundamental to the Gnostic doctrine, it is at the very heart of its metaphysics. The innumerable pairs of opposites in the Gnostic texts include: the Pleroma/the world, emptiness/fullness, being/non-being, Mother/Father, light/dark, god/devil, good/evil, above/below, male/female, living/dead, healthy/sick, waking/ sleeping, drunk/sober, virgin/whore, freedom/slavery, motion/rest, visible/invisible, known/unknowable, and so on. As noted, in Gnostic cosmogony, creation comes into being through a process of emanation of paired opposites. Each successive emanation results in a pair of opposites which is not only further removed from the Pleroma than the previous pair, but is also more differentiated. At the level of the created world, the opposites are fully differentiated so that their underlying unity is often not recognised. The opposites are not just part of life in this world, they are fundamental to it. No opposites, no world.

* * *

As noted above, dualism is at the very heart of PKD's "two source" Gnostic cosmogony in which creation is the result of the dialectic interaction of the opposing poles of the primal syzygy. He claims a "great war is being fought at this moment between God and [the devil]. The fate of the universe is at stake, its actual physical existence" (2008, p. 243). However, despite being central to his cosmogony, the nature of the opposites intrinsic to that dualism, and the interaction of those opposites, does not receive that same comprehensive and profound treatment as it does in Jung's work. The theme of the opposites, along with the accompanying need for their reconciliation and integration, is the cornerstone of Jung's worldview, and, as such, it is the principal tenet of analytical psychology. The theme of the opposites is the crucial leitmotif running through the entire Jungian corpus, principally in his final major work, which he credited as being his magnum opus, *Mysterium Coniunctionis* (1955–56).

Jung's psychology of the opposites is founded on its metaphysical antecedent, as articulated in Jung's Gnostic vision, *The Seven Sermons*. Somewhat paradoxically, the opposites do not, in fact, exist in the emptiness of the Pleroma as they cancel one another out. Yet, to the extent that they can be considered to exist at all, in the fullness of the Pleroma, the opposites exist in a harmonious state of equilibrium. The process of differentiation separates the opposites so that the resulting energy tension between the poles of the opposites allows creation to come into being. Consequently, there are, in effect, three states of differentiation in Jung's Gnostic vision: a) wholly undifferentiated, cancelled out, opposites in the emptiness of the Pleroma; b) somewhat differentiated opposites within the fullness of the Pleroma, which become increasingly differentiated, the further they have emanated from the source of the Pleroma; and c) wholly differentiated opposites in the created world. In Jung's view, existence is founded on the principle of the opposites; nothing can exist without a balancing opposite (McGuire & Shamdasani, 2012). Without differentiation, creation is an inherent potential of the Pleroma only, and the opposites remain in a state of equipoise which Jung described as an absolute coincidence of opposites (1951). This is key to understanding the metaphysics of the ancient Gnostics, of Jung—and, to a lesser extent, of PKD. The created world is predicated on the differentiation of the opposites. This is the crux of Gnostic cosmogony.

Crucial to Jung's psychology of the opposites is that the non-differentiated state of the opposites is the equivalent of unconsciousness.

Without the differentiation of opposites there can be no consciousness. Influenced by Eckhart, Jung claims that God differentiates itself from the essentially unconscious, undifferentiated Godhead, and the resulting dialectic between God and Godhead leads to consciousness (ibid.). In the same way that the differentiation of opposites leads to creation in Jung's Gnostic metaphysics, differentiation also leads to the creation of consciousness in his psychology. Both Jung's Gnostic metaphysics and his psychology can be summarised as: the non-differentiation of the opposites is unconsciousness; the differentiation of opposites is consciousness. If the opposites are not differentiated, then creation risks dissolution in the Pleroma. If the opposites are not differentiated psychologically, a person is in peril of succumbing to what Jung considered to be the sin of unconsciousness. Whereas the Gnostic sought the dissolution of the opposites, hence a return to the Pleroma, Jung's psychology seeks the opposite; the reconciliation and integration of the fully differentiated opposites, and a more fully conscious wholeness.

Another fundamental insight of Jung's Gnostic vision is the danger of favouring one pole of a pair of opposites over its complementary opposite pole. Whereas in Gnostic cosmogony, Sophia's conception without her male consort (i.e., an imbalance of the male/female syzygy) caused a rupturing of cosmic wholeness that led to the creation of our fallen world, an imbalance of the opposites, at a psychological level, results in a split in the psyche and a loss of psychological wholeness. The two poles of a pair of opposites may appear phenomenally distinct, but their essence is fundamentally one. Even in creation, where the opposites are rent asunder, that is, are wholly differentiated, they retain their underlying unity. Phenomenally, the nature of the opposites in creation is *differentiated yet inextricably united*. There is no hot without cold, no light without dark, and so on. Ultimately, the opposites can never be truly separated: they issue from a single root. Noting that there are as many nights as there are days, and that one is as long as the other over the course of the year, Jung's view was that a happy life would need to be counterbalanced by a measure of darkness. Indeed, both happiness and sadness, like all other polar opposites, are only meaningful in relation to one another. The essential nature of the opposites is always both/and, rather than, either/or. As the Chinese philosopher, Lao Tze (605 BCE–531 BCE), put it: "Without Darkness, there can be no Light." Where the optimist sees the glass as half full, and the pessimist sees it as half empty, Jung, and the Gnostics (and the Taoists), realise that it cannot be one without the other. We cannot have one pole of a pair of opposites without the other, and to the extent that we strive exclusively for one pole, we unavoidably fall under the spell of its counterpart. The person who appears to have one pole without its balancing twin is psychologically sick due to the imbalance (Jung, 2009). The rejected pole is forced down into the unconscious where it forms part of the shadow, from where it largely plays out autonomously, resulting in effects that can range from the mildly neurotic to the catastrophic. The fullness of the Pleroma, encompassing all that is, contains both poles, the light and the dark, the good and the evil. Similarly, psychological wholeness demands the acceptance of both poles. The essential need to reconcile the opposites and maintain them in a state of equilibrium became a fundamental maxim of Jung's psychology. Here can be found a correspondence with the teachings of Buddhism. Along with ignorance, attachment and aversion form the three poisons in Buddhism. Like his Buddhist counterparts, Jung exhorts us to walk the middle path between the opposites, being neither too attached, nor averse, to either pole. An imbalanced conscious position will invoke a compensatory unconscious counter position due to the self-regulatory nature of the psyche. If the inner psychological state is not made conscious, in other words, if the conscious and unconscious counter poles are not reconciled, then, out of necessity, the unresolved conflict will be encountered in the outer world in what is generally regarded as fate (Jung, 1951).

CHAPTER FIVE

Archons and archetypes

For we wrestle not against flesh and blood, but against principalities, against powers, against the rulers of the darkness of this world, against spiritual wickedness in high places.

—Ephesians 6:12, KJV

In sharp contrast to the Judaeo-Christian tradition which teaches that God created this world, the Gnostics maintained that this world was created, not by a transcendent, ultimate divinity, but by Sophia's bastard child, the demiurge, and his minions, the archons. *Archon* is the English form of the Greek word, *arkhōn*, which simply means "lord" or "ruler". In the Gnostic tradition, the archons were created by the demiurge to rule over the material world and its human inhabitants. In the Nag Hammadi Library the only text dedicated exclusively to the subject of the archons is *The Reality of the Rulers* (alternatively, *The Nature of the Rulers*, or *The Hypostasis of the Archons*). According to scholar of Sethian Gnosticism, John D. Turner (2007), the clear implication of the title is that the "rulers" in Gnostic cosmology, the demiurge and his archons, are, in fact, to be considered real. As Jung would reiterate two millennia later concerning the reality of evil, the Gnostics took the existence of the archons as substantively real.

In *The Secret Book of John*, Sophia, the last and lowest of the aeons to emanate from the Pleroma, wants to conceive a thought from herself. However, she does so without the approval of the Spirit, and without the consent of her male counterpart. The resulting bastard child was imperfect and misshapen. He is described as ignorant darkness having the body of a snake and the head of a lion (Figure 5). Ashamed at what she had done, Sophia rejects her offspring and casts it out of the Pleroma where none of the other aeons can see it. She enshrouds it in a cloud so that only the Holy Spirit, the Mother of the Living, could see it. She calls her child Yaldabaoth. In his turn, Yaldabaoth, the demiurge, united with the thoughtlessness (*aponoia*) within him and created the archons. Lacking the light of the Spirit from above, Yaldabaoth and the archons created the first human being after the image of God, but with the likeness of themselves, so that the human would give them light. The archons fashioned the physical body of the human, but for a long time he was inanimate and unable to move. In the meantime, Sophia had repented and wanted to recover the power she lost when conceiving the demiurge. Subsequently, angels from on high are sent down who advise the demiurge to breathe the spirit, which he had obtained from his mother, Sophia, into the face of the first human so that he would rise up. The demiurge did so because he is ignorant and, as a result, lost his power to humanity. Jealous that the first human was more intelligent and enlightened than they were, as well as lacking in evil, the archons cast the human into the depths of the material world. In short, the key point is that the demiurge and the archons created humanity in order to provide them with what they lacked, the light of the Holy Spirit. Humanity was created as food for the archons.

Smith (2008) describes the archons as the "ghastly counterparts of the spiritual aeons … malicious minions of the demiurge" (p. 22) and goes on to note that the bastard child symbolism of the demiurge is appropriate in two ways. Not only is he illegitimate in the sense of having no father, he is also illegitimate in the sense that something is fundamentally wrong with his existence. This defect is the disruption to the harmonious balance of the opposites in the Pleroma symbolised by the male/female imbalance when Sophia conceived without her male counterpart. The disharmony is further symbolised by the fact that the bodies of the archons are hermaphroditic. They are both male and female, yet not fully either, indicating that the harmony of the male/female syzygy has been disturbed and the opposites are beginning to split.

The Revelation of Adam teaches that the demiurge and the archons "angrily divided us" (Meyer, 2007, p. 347). Consequently, we became two beings, that is, male and female. Thus, the archons are responsible for the severing of the original androgynous unity of the Pleroma into the duality of the created world. Having been created by the offspring of the last aeon, Sophia, the archons are far removed from the source of the Pleroma, and inhabit a liminal space within its lowest reaches, just on the cusp of the created world. As a result, the archons encroach upon, and have effect within, our world. According to *The First Revelation of James*, this world is the dwelling place of many archons.

Perceptively, as well as somewhat politically, the scholar of Gnosticism, Nicola D. Lewis (2013), notes that the word "archon" is derived from the Greek work for a *political* ruler, and also notes that the language in the Gnostic texts used to describe "those who oppress us through enslaving our minds and hijacking our appetites is also political" (p. 135). (The use of the word "appetites" seems apropos given that the archons feed off us.) She suggests that the Gnostics' use of the term "archon" might convey a deeply political message, and that the Gnostics' view was that our enemies are "those in high places". Were the Gnostics—and perhaps Lewis—alluding to the idea that the archons control, deceive, defile, and imprison humanity through the agency of those in high political office? *The Reality of the* Rulers quotes St. Paul who taught that our struggle is not against the flesh, but against the authorities of the world, and the spirits of wickedness in high places. There are some commentators, the ones who are invariably dismissed as "conspiracy theorists", who claim that there is a hidden agenda by a nefarious secret government that seeks the total enslavement of humanity. The Gnostics would disagree; humanity has always been born into slavery. The Matrix that is our reality has already been pulled over our eyes to blind us from the truth.

One of the fundamental points that should be noted about the archons is that their powers are limited. *The Reality of the Rulers* teaches is that it is a mistake to think that the archons have power over us. The archons do not have the capability to "overpower the root of truth" (Meyer, 2007, p. 196). The text states that Incorruptibility looked down from above and the archons of the darkness became enamoured by her image reflected in the waters below. However, they were powerless to seize hold of her because they merely have a soul, and those with soul cannot take hold of those that have spirit. The archons cannot defile the Gnostics who have realised their spiritual essence, and made their home within the Incorruptibility of the Pleroma where the virgin Spirit dwells, a Spirit which is superior to the archons and the chaos of their corrupt world. For the Gnostics, the seed of the Pleroma within each person is more powerful than the agents of darkness, and those who live from the place of pure (virgin) Spirit, and abide in truth, are beyond the influence of the archons. "Blessed are the pure in heart: for they shall see God" (Matthew 5:8, KJV). Lewis (2013) comments that, whereas the archons "can harm us, oppress us, violate us, imprison, and enslave us" (p. 135), they can enact their violence only on our bodies; they cannot harm our spirit. It might be added that, in addition to our bodies, the archons can equally, and far more significantly, harm our minds and our souls. The spirit, on the other hand, is immaculate, immune, incorruptible, and immortal.

Due to their limited powers, the archons need to control humanity through deception. For example, *The Gospel of Philip* teaches that the archons wanted to fool people because they were jealous of humanity's kinship with what is truly good. Therefore, in an act of deception, they took the names of the good and assigned them to what is not good in order to link good names to what is not good. They do this in order to take free people and enslave them. In PKD's view, the power of the archons is nothing more than "mere occlusion" (2008). It is said that the devil's greatest achievement was in persuading people to think that he did not exist. The same could be said for the demiurge and the archons.

* * *

The Gnostic demiurge and the archons are not explicitly referenced in the *Seven Sermons*. However, the figure of the demiurge appears indirectly in Jung's representation of the Gnostic God *Abraxas*, whom Jung reintroduces in response to the dead—to whom the *Seven Sermons* are addressed—when they ask to be given instruction on the subject of God. Jung borrows the name Abraxas from Basilides, considered to be one of the great Gnostic teachers from the second century, and to whom Jung pseudo-epigraphically attributes the *Seven Sermons*. Only fragments of Basilides's writings survive and, as a consequence, little is known about either the man or his teachings, and this may be one of the reasons that Jung's Abraxas differs markedly from the few extant details of the one presented by Basilides. For Basilides, Abraxas was the leader of the lowest class of angelic beings, which had emanated from the Pleroma (Rudolph, 1987), and was considered to be wholly good. On the other hand, Jung, despite having been influenced by what little is known of Basilides, presents a refashioned Abraxas in the *Seven Sermons*, the God that humanity had forgotten, or perhaps more accurately, disavowed. For Jung, Abraxas is the highest god—although not to be confused with the ultimate Godhead, the Pleroma—and the first emanation from the Pleroma in Jung's system. A curiously ambiguous figure, Abraxas is a double nature in one, embodying both good, represented by God, as well as evil, represented by the devil. Jung felt that the one-sided (i.e., wholly God) God-image of Judaeo-Christianity was incomplete and could no more stand than a one-legged chair. According to Jung, for a God-image to be real it needed a compensating shadow because anything real casts a shadow. The image of God casts a shadow, the devil, which is as great as itself. For Jung, both God and devil were real, and there cannot be one without the other. Created as much as creator, Abraxas is distinct from the ultimate Godhead and yet cannot be wholly identified with the world either, and therefore, like the archons, exists in the liminal space between the Pleroma and creation. For Jung, Abraxas is the demiurge.

As noted above, Jung's Gnostic cosmogony is founded on the differentiation of opposites and, as a somewhat, but perhaps not quite wholly, created being, Abraxas is no different, coming into existence as the pairing of God and devil. Jung describes the polar opposites of the nature of Abraxas as nothing and everything, eternal emptiness and eternal fullness, eternal darkness and eternal brightness, above and below, old and young, yes and no. Unlike the syzygies of the Pleroma, however, in which the opposites cancel one another out, God and devil stand opposed to one another within the figure of Abraxas. Another important polar opposition embodied within Abraxas, and one that further differentiates Jung's Abraxas from the Gnostic demiurge, is that, in addition to being an emanated being from the Pleroma above, Abraxas is, simultaneously, a "monster of the underworld" (Jung, 2009, p. 521), with an inferior consciousness and a primitive awareness, and which rises up from the depths of the unconscious. Furthermore, Jung identifies the quality of "effectiveness" as both the differentiator as well as the link that unites God and devil in the figure of Abraxas. It is this effectiveness of Abraxas that gives both God and devil the ability to have effect within the created world. Symbolically, Abraxas is typically represented with the head of a rooster, a human body, and the tail of a snake (Figure 10). Thus, Abraxas is a figure that embodies and unites the opposites, God and devil, good and evil, Heaven and Earth: opposites which collide in the experience of being human.

Jung believed that, rather than being a theological construct, or a mere metaphysical speculation beyond the realm of human experience, Abraxas, as a god who was effective within creation, could be experienced within the psyche. Such an encounter Jung described as *numinous*, however, rather than referring to an experience of a transcendent ultimate realty, he meant an experience that welled up from the depths of the unconscious (Stein, 2014). To experience the numinous is to be confronted by a *mysterium tremendum et fascinans* (an awful and fascinating mystery), both awesome and awful in equal measure. To encounter Abraxas is to experience the numinous in all its awful mystery.

Mindful of the need to accept both sides of the opposites, Jung claimed that Abraxas is to be respected for both the fascination he evokes as well as all his awful mystery. Given that he is two-natures-in-one,

Figure 10. The Gnostic god Abraxas.

both God and devil, Abraxas is to not to be feared or loved, yet, para-doxically, both feared and loved (Jung, 2009). Yet, Abraxas is neither to be sought after nor rejected since, like the archons' veil of deception—and the Matrix—Abraxas surrounds us on all sides and will seek us out. Instead, Jung advocates a middle way balanced between the poles of the opposites: a path he likens to being crucified accompanied by the fear of being overpowered (ibid.). In Jung's Gnostic vision, crucifixion means to be stretched out between the poles of the opposites.

* * *

Despite the fact that there is no mention of the archons in the *Seven Sermons*, a parallel can be drawn between them and Jung's psychological concept of the *archetype*. Stratford (2007) describes the archons, in their psychological aspect, as the "… forces which keep us in the artificially constructed system; the false reality of television and titillation and cor-ruption and consumerism and greed. The archons are 'the powers that be'; all those ideas which separate us from living wholly and truthfully, from social justice, from compassion" (p. 45). In the words of St. Paul:

> For that which I do I allow not: for what I would, that do I not; but what I hate, that do I. If then I do that which I would not, I consent unto the law that it is good. Now then it is no more I that do it, but sin that dwelleth in me. For I know that in me (that is, in my flesh) dwelleth no good thing: for to will is present with me; but how to perform that which is good I find not. For the good that I would I do not: but the evil which I would not, that I do. (Romans 7:15–19, KJV)

Psychologically, the archons are all those forces that prevent us from doing the things we want to or know we should do, and compel us to do the things we do not want to or know that we should not. Those forces are the negative aspects of the archetypes. In Jungian psychol-ogy an *archetype* (from the Greek, *archétypon*, meaning primitive model, or original pattern), is a primordial, universal mental image thought to have been inherited from humanity's earliest ancestors and consid-ered to exist in the collective unconscious, and therefore accessible, albeit indirectly, by an individual psyche. In very simplistic terms, the archetypes are to human psychology what the instincts are to human biology; however, this hardly does justice to the concept. Although they cannot be experienced directly, the archetypes exert their influence from the depths of the collective unconscious and predispose an individual to behave in particular ways. In short, the archetypes are the psychological blueprints that pattern human behaviour.

Crucial to understanding Jung's concept of the archetypes is that they can only provide form, rather than content, to human experience. The archetype provides the psychological pattern, and the individual's subjective experience fills it in. It is the empty pattern of the archetype that is inherited from the collective unconscious and not the content. For example, under the influence of the hero archetype a person might feel compelled to act, well, heroically. If this psychological urge is not acted on then the psyche might respond with a compensating dream of the hero, however, it will not be the hero archetype *per se* appearing in the dream but a symbolic representation of it in the form of a specific hero, such as James Bond for one person, and Alexander the Great for another. For Jung, there was a distinction between the archetype-as-such and the multifarious representative expressions it could have in an individual psyche.

Jung's archetypal theory has its roots not only in Plato's theory of Ideas and Forms, but, perhaps more significantly, also in German philosopher Immanuel Kant's (1724–1804) reasoning on the distinction between *phenomenon* and *noumenon*. Kant viewed the noumenon, the essential thing-in-itself, as a wholly transcendent object that is entirely unknowable by the senses but can only be apprehended by reason. In contrast, the phenomenon is the thing, or a representation of the thing, as it can be perceived by the senses. For Kant, there was a fundamental and irreconcilable difference between the two. As I argued in my previous work (Douglas, 2016), there are clear parallels between Jung's archetype-as-such and Kant's noumenon, and between the representation of an archetype as it appears to consciousness and Kant's phenomenon. However, a fundamental difference between Kant's and Jung's theories must be noted. Whereas, for Kant, the distance between the noumenon and the phenomenon cannot be bridged, for Jung, the archetype-as-such is paradoxically both unknowable in its essence, but simultaneously knowable through its representative expression in the psyche. In other words, the archetype can only be experienced indirectly.

In Jung's archetypal theory, all archetypes have their positive and negative aspects (1951), and are thus capable of exerting both beneficial and/or detrimental effects. In the same way that the aeons and archons constitute the fullness of the Pleroma, the archetypes constitute the collective unconscious. In other words, the aeons and the archons of Gnostic systems can be considered to be the corresponding spiritual, or metaphysical, counterparts of the psychological archetypes, and therefore able to exert an influence on the human psyche, indirectly shaping, if not controlling, human experience. Jung himself thought so. In his "Psychological Commentary on 'The Tibetan Book of the Great Liberation'" (1954), he states that the gods are archetypal thought-forms whose peaceful and wrathful aspects symbolise the opposites, that is, the polar opposites of positive and negative are united in one and the same figure. Jung's view is that this has a direct parallel with psychological experience in which there is no position without its corresponding negation. "Where there is faith, there is doubt; where there is doubt, there is credulity; where there is morality, there is temptation. Only saints have diabolic visions" (p. 123). The opposites define one another; they are one and the same thing. For all intents and purposes, the collective unconscious—and its denizens, the archetypes, in both their positive and negative aspects—is, in *essence*, one and the same thing as the fullness of the Pleroma.

* * *

Like the Gnostics with their concept of the ruling authorities, the demiurge and the archons who keep an enslaved humanity imprisoned in the created world, PKD also thought that our world was controlled by maleficent authorities who impose on us "pseudo-realities" through the means of "very sophisticated electronic mechanisms" (1978). In a paper with a typically quirky title, "How to Build a Universe that Doesn't Fall Apart Two Days Later" (ibid.), PKD feels that, having conjured up entire imaginary universes in his science fiction novels—universes that do not fall apart two days later—he is eminently qualified to assert that the ruling authorities have an astonishing power to create false universes in the human mind. Writing in his *Exegesis*, he clarifies that, in accordance with his acosmic perspective, we are not so much enslaved in a false world, because there is no world there, but, rather, we are enslaved by a very real and evil entity. For PKD, we live in a fallen world, into which we have been cast, and where we have become puppets at the mercy of an unseen puppeteer who is anything but God. As a result, we are compelled to live out our lives "upon a contrived stage" (2011, loc. 6780). In one entry in the *Exegesis* PKD ponders what purpose this world serves but concludes, on that particular occasion, that he does not care, but that it is sufficient to realise that its purpose is not for our benefit, and we need to be rescued from it. However, in Gnostic fashion, he does allow himself to speculate that we are nothing more than an energy source used to power this fallen world (loc. 6728).

Elsewhere in his *Exegesis*, PKD recounts a dream of a farming family of which the children are referred to as the "spinners". The farmland is very old and has become contaminated with heavy metals and the poisoning effect is causing the children to go blind. A young boy looks through a thick magnifying glass at the sun which he can just manage to see. Soon he will be totally blind. PKD interprets the spinners to be immortals who came to this world and became poisoned and lost the faculty of the third eye—the ability to see other worlds—hence the need for the very thick magnifying glass. The sun is a symbol for Christ and the boy's great difficulty in seeing the sun/Christ, and ultimate blindness, means the people can no longer read sacred scripture. God has not stopped transmitting his message, but the lights have dimmed, the people are going blind, and are no longer able to perceive the divine revelation (loc. 13913). Alternatively, the spinners could be seen as the spinners of this world, in other words, the archons. The Gnostic demiurge is considered to be blind—one of his epithets is Samael, meaning "blind God"—further linking the spinners and the blind child with the demiurge and the archons. This suggests that not only are we trapped in a toxic world, unable to see our way out, we are also responsible for having created it. This theme that we are also the archons, simultaneously the creator of the prison, the prison wardens, and the prisoners, is a theme that pervades much of the *Exegesis*; for example, "The ruled is that which rules" (loc. 6815).

The Gnostics saw the world differently than we do today. They believed that to be born into this world is to be imprisoned by the archons; to depart from this world is to be liberated. Whereas we are taught to celebrate life and to mourn death, perhaps the Gnostics would have taught the opposite; that we should mourn birth into enslavement, and celebrate liberation from the archons' prison. The notion of this world as a prison will be explored more fully in the next chapter.

CHAPTER SIX

The cave and the prison

"But I don't want to go among mad people," Alice remarked. "Oh, you can't help that," said the Cat: "we're all mad here. I'm mad. You're mad." "How do you know I'm mad?" said Alice. "You must be," said the Cat, "or you wouldn't have come here."

—Lewis Carroll, *Alice in Wonderland*

One of the defining characteristics of the Gnostic tradition is that humanity has been imprisoned in the material world by the archons through an act of deception. This is a recurring motif throughout a number of texts in the Nag Hammadi Library. For example, *The Secret Book of John* describes this world as the shadow of death in which the human body is a tomb. This body-tomb has been created from the four elements of earth, water, fire, and wind, which the text redefines as matter, darkness, desire, and the artificial spirit respectively. Once created, humanity was then bound by the veil of forgetfulness, and enslaved in the material world. Indeed, the archons enslaved not only humanity, but the "whole of creation" from the very beginning up to the present day. *The Gospel of Philip* notes that the archons, resentful of humans' affinity with the Pleroma and envious of the light that had been bestowed on them, wanted to take free people and, through an act of deception, enslave them for eternity. Likewise, the *Authoritative Discourse* refers to an adversary who attempts to beguile humans with hidden poisons and bind them in slavery, whereas, although lacking the idea of the deceit of the archons, *The Tripartite Tractate* nevertheless contrasts the freedom of the Pleroma with the created world which is ruled by ignorance, and characterised by captivity, obsequiousness, and suffering. In a not dissimilar vein, *The Gospel of Thomas* simply notes the saviour's astonishment that the great wealth of the human spirit has come to dwell in the poverty of the human body.

In that most Gnostic of Gnostic-themed motion pictures, *The Matrix*, Morpheus tells Neo that the Matrix is nothing more than a computer-generated dream world designed by the machines (i.e., the archons), in order to enslave humanity and turn it into an energy source for the machines. Morpheus holds up a battery to emphasis his point graphically. This is a crucial, yet invariably overlooked, Gnostic theme, and this scene from *The Matrix* captures it perfectly. As noted above, in the most Gnostic of Gnostic cosmogonies, *The Secret Book of John*, the archons created this world, and keep us enslaved in it, in order to feed off of us. They lacked the light of the Pleroma and, therefore, wanted to create a human in the image of God so that the light of God reflected in his image (i.e., the human) could illuminate them. In other words, the archons created humanity as an energy source. The archons are energy parasites who feed off us! The agenda of the archons could not have been captured any better than when Don Juan Matus, the teacher of Carlos Castaneda, states that,

> We have a predator that came from the depths of the cosmos and took over the rule of our lives. Human beings are its prisoners. The predator is our lord and master. It has rendered us docile, helpless. If we want to protest, it suppresses our protest. If we want to act independently, it demands that we don't do so. *They took us over because we are food for them, and they squeeze us mercilessly because we are their sustenance.* Just as we rear chickens in coops … the predators raise us in human coops. … Therefore, their food is always available to them. (Castaneda, 2017, emphasis added)

Trapped in a chicken coop as a food source for the archons is not something most humans would take lying down—one would think—hence the need for the deception with which the archons keep humanity imprisoned. Indeed, it's a bitter pill to swallow—it must have been red—and perhaps that is why so many people take the blue pill, even if they have occasionally peeked through the veil and obtained a taste of what reality is. As Morpheus put it, they wake up in their beds having seen a little of the dream world they are trapped in, and they believe whatever it is they want to believe. More accurately, they believe whatever the archons deceive them into believing. According to PKD (2008), our world is under a spell in which we are either in a state of sleep, or in a trance, in which something is causing us to "... see what it wants us to see and remember and think what it wants us to remember and think. Which means we're whatever it wants us to be. Which in turn means that we have no genuine existence. We're at the mercy of some kind of whim" (p. 188).

Platonism is considered to be one of the origins of the Gnostic tradition (Pearson, 2007) and a clear parallel can be seen between Plato's "Allegory of the Cave" and the Gnostic view of humanity imprisoned in the world. In Plato's allegory, which appears in Book VII of *The Republic*—a short extract of which appears in the Nag Hammadi Library—a group of human troglodytes have spent their entire lives as prisoners chained against a wall in such a way that they can only look at a blank wall of the cave. Behind and above them is a fire, and in front of the fire, but behind the wall, other people pass carrying a variety of objects in much the same way as puppeteers hide behind a screen and hold their puppets above the screen where their audience can see them. The shadows of these puppeteers cannot be seen by the prisoners, but the shadows of the objects they carry are projected onto the wall of the cave where they can be seen by the prisoners. The sounds made by the people carrying the objects echo off the wall on which the shadows are projected giving the prisoners the impression that the shadows are making the sounds. Having never seen anything else, the prisoners mistake their world of shadows for reality. Nor do they realise that the shadows are based on an actuality beyond their vision. Likewise, the Gnostics considered humanity to be like Plato's cave-dwellers, imprisoned in an illusory world of darkness. At some point, one of the prisoners is freed from his shackles and turns to see the fire and the objects. His eyes are stinging due to the dazzling light of the fire and, unable to properly perceive the objects, he struggles to accept that the objects are, in fact, real, and that the shadows, which he previously mistook as real, are unreal. Confused and in pain, he returns to the false reality of the shadows that he is accustomed to and which he has grown comfortable with despite his imprisonment. Subsequently, he is dragged out of the cave into the light of day where he is blinded by the sun's radiance. In pain and shock he is initially angry at this radical change in circumstance. Gradually his eyes adjust to the light and to his new reality and he realises its superiority to the cave. Now in pity at the plight of the prisoners he left behind he returns to the cave to help them escape. However, having acclimatised to the light of day he is, once again, blinded, this time by the shadows. The other prisoners then conclude from his blindness that his journey outside the cave has adversely affected him and cannot believe his claims of the glory of the upper world. Consequently, the other prisoners would choose the prison of the cave rather than the freedom of the outside world. Indeed, they would kill anyone who tried to drag them out of the cave. Like one of these other prisoners in Plato's cave, one of the characters in *The Matrix*, Cypher, does not want to escape from the computer-generated enslavement of the matrix. Instead, he chooses the pseudo-bliss of ignorance rather than face his predicament. Like the prisoner who escaped the cave and saw the light, Cypher knows the reality of the dream world that holds him captive, yet he would rather stay. Like a computer-era Judas he betrays Morpheus, and chooses to remain a prisoner … provided he forgets, and he receives his thirty pieces of silver, which in Cypher's case, is to become someone rich and important, like an actor, who gets to dine out on steak in fancy restaurants, even though, at the time of selling his soul, he knows it will all be an illusion. Cypher is human, it should be remembered, and the human species is not the finest handiwork in the universe—it was fashioned by the demiurge and the archons after all. It consists of individuals who are not the sharpest tools in the cosmic shed and have an incorrigible tendency to listen to any snake-oil salesman who tells them what they want to believe. Would you like some more blue pills with your steak, sir? Cypher wanted to be a famous actor. Perhaps those that endlessly fawn over the latest Hollywood starlets are just like Cypher; collaborating with jailers to perpetuate their living death in the world of shadows.

* * *

Like the Gnostics—and Plato—before him, PKD's metaphysics postulates that our world is a prison. According to PKD, this is a tragic realm in which we are prisoners, and the ultimate tragedy is that we do not even realise it. We have always been enslaved, but mistakenly assume that we are free because we have never known what it means to be free. "*This is a prison* ... a metal world. Driven by cogs, a machine that grinds along, dealing out suffering and death" (Dick, 2008, p. 133, emphasis in original). However, the archons have an endless ability to conjure up all kinds of prisons, "subtle ones and gross ones, prisons within prisons; prisons for the body, and, worse by far, prisons for the mind" (p. 231). In his *Exegesis* he views this world as being ruled by malevolent forces, and subject to what he terms "astral determinism". He refers to this jailhouse as the "Black Iron Prison" (BIP), an insidious and oppressive form of human control, permeating not just our world but the whole of time and space (Dick, 2011, loc. 4868). Like the Matrix, the BIP is everywhere, completely surrounding us. We can see it outside our windows, and we can see it on our televisions—especially on our television. Like Neo, we are slaves of the BIP, born into captivity and enslaved in a prison of the mind that we cannot discern by means of smell, taste, or touch. Describing the BIP by way of analogy, PKD states that if the universe is considered to be a conscious psyche, then the BIP would be a "rigid ossified complex" (ibid., loc. 6806), a complex that cannot evolve and knows only chaos and decay, and which is destined to repeat the same thought, over and over, as if it was on an endless loop. That thought is the enforcement of the BIP state in which we are trapped. The BIP is a merciless world from which we need to be saved. (Interestingly, in an act of synchronicity, I came across the reference to the BIP as an endlessly repeating thought on what is known as Groundhog Day, February 2, 2016, a day popularised by the eponymous 1993 film in which the protagonist is condemned to relive the same day, day after day, until he learns how to break the cycle.) In the *Tractates* PKD also refers to "the Empire", a reference to the tyranny of the Roman Empire which he believes continues to this day, albeit in different form. The Empire is, in effect, a metonym for the BIP. He describes the Empire as "the institution, the codification, of derangement" (2001, p. 264), an insane organisation that inflicts its insanity on humanity by enforcing the BIP through violence, since violence is its nature. Elsewhere in the *Tractates* he associates the Empire with "undeserved suffering, chaos, and death" (p. 267). According to PKD, the BIP has existed throughout time, or is, perhaps, outside time altogether, and that everyone who has ever lived has been imprisoned within the iron walls of a prison without even realising it (ibid.). In what became a catchphrase of the *Tractates*, PKD declares that the "Empire never ended", in other words, we are still enslaved by the Empire in the BIP, or, in the words of the Gnostics, we are all enslaved by the archons in a fallen world. PKD's concept of the BIP, and the fact that the "nice" world we see instead is, in fact, a delusion, was inspired, like most of his metaphysics—Gnostic or otherwise—by his 2-3-74 experience.

In his *Tractates* PKD contrasts the BIP with what he terms the "Palm Tree Garden" (PTG). Without citing his source, he claims the Gnostics believed in two temporal aeons: the first, or current time, characterised by evil, and the second, to come in the future, which would be benign. The first he calls the "Age of Iron" and is represented by the BIP, and the second, the "Age of Gold", represented by the PTG. (He also claims that the Age of Iron ended in August 1974 and was replaced by the PTG. This is somewhat at odds with the claim that the Empire [BIP] never ended. However, this is the mind of PKD; it is rarely logical, and not always consistent. That is, no doubt, a large part of his appeal.) In terms of its essence—rather than its temporality—the BIP is a metaphor for the material world, in other words, the counterfeit world created by the archons who tried, and failed, to mimic the aeonic realms of the Pleroma, and who use their creation to enslave humanity. On the other hand, the PTG represents, but is not identical with, the indestructible, incorruptible, aeonic realm, that is, the Pleroma. One counterfeit, the other real. Now the upper (yang) and lower (yin) realms of PKD's two-source Gnostic cosmogony, noted above (Figure 7), can be replaced, or alternatively represented, by the Palm Tree Garden and the Black Iron Prison (Figure 11).

Figure 11. The Palm Tree Garden and the Black Iron Prison.

Elsewhere, PKD describes the PTG as a "park of peace and beauty" (1977), a world far superior to the BIP that it will, ultimately, replace. In this variation of his schema, the BIP world has passed and we now live in an intermediate world in which the oppression of humanity, and the endless war that invariably accompanies it, have, to some extent, been mitigated. Then there is an alternative world, superimposed over this one, which will come into being in the future when "the correct variables in our past have been reprogrammed" (ibid.). When we awaken to this new world it will be as if we have always lived there, and the current, intermediate world, along with the BIP will have been "eradicated mercifully" (ibid.) from our minds.

Regardless of whether we live in the BIP proper, or the intermediate, BIP-lite, PKD, like the Gnostics before him, clearly believed that our world remains a prison imposed by nefarious forces. The Empire has not ended, at least, not yet. We are still surrounded by, and trapped in, the Matrix.

CHAPTER SEVEN

The dream and the hologram

How can you prove whether at this moment we are sleeping, and all
our thoughts are a dream; or whether we are awake, and talking to one
another in the waking state?

—Plato

The two fundamental characteristics of the Gnostic view that the material world was created by the demiurge and the archons are that: a) it is a prison, and b) that the archons keep humans enslaved by deluding them into thinking that the material world is real when it is, in fact, according to the Gnostics, an illusion. Whereas the previous chapter dealt with the world-as-prison, this chapter turns to the concept of the world-as-illusion.

In *The Matrix* Morpheus asks Neo if he had ever had a dream that he was sure was real. He questions Neo further by adding that, if he were unable to wake from that dream, how would he be able to distinguish between the dream world and the world of our normal waking state, that is, the world which we assume to be the "real" world. On the same topic, the British medical doctor Havelock Ellis (1859–1939) claimed that dreams appear real, and, for all intents and purposes, might be considered real, for as long as they last, and that we could say no more about the waking state of consensual, so-called reality. Similarly, the Gnostic texts of the Nag Hammadi Library make it clear that this world is an illusion that we have been deceived into taking for reality. For example, *The Treatise on Resurrection* cautions against thinking that the resurrection is an illusion given that the goal of the Gnostic is to be released from the fetters of matter. It declares that it is this world, rather than resurrection from it, that is the illusion; an illusion in which the rich have become poor, or, in the words of *The Gospel of Thomas*, the richness of spirit has become trapped in the poverty of the material world. Elsewhere, the notion of being asleep is a recurring trope of the Gnostic texts, used to describe the deluded state of mistaking this world for reality. In *The Reality of the Rulers*, the archons cause a deep sleep (i.e., ignorance) to fall upon the first human before he is cast down into the material realm. Subsequently, humanity is asleep and ignorant of its entrapment in matter. When humans sleep, they dream, and *The Revelation of Adam* occurs while he is asleep, that is, it comes to him in a dream, and it encourages him to awaken from the "sleep of death" (Meyer, 2007, p. 344). As Einstein's oft-quoted aphorism points out, reality is merely an illusion, albeit a very persistent one. For the Gnostics, this world is a shadowy phantasm, about which the archons keep us perpetually in the dark. We are controlled by the archons because they control the false reality we are living in. However, according to the Gnostics, the archons are effectively powerless and their power over us exists only to the extent that they can deceive us into thinking that the false reality is actually real.

This notion is powerfully representing in the spoon-bending scene in *The Matrix* in which Neo encounters a boy with a shaved head who appears like a Buddhist monk. Lying in front of the boy are a number of bent spoons and he currently holds another which he is bending through the power of thought. He hands a straight spoon to Neo with the implied suggestion that he should try to bend it with his mind. As Neo takes the spoon, the boy tells him that he should not try to bend the spoon because that is impossible. Rather, he should simply try to realise the truth. "What truth?" asks Neo. The boy replies that there is no spoon, and it is not the spoon that bends, but only oneself that bends. Neo then turns his attention to the spoon, which now mirrors the whole room. As he stares at it, it starts to bend. This suggests that when we realise the truth and "bend", that is, transform in the light of the realised truth and awaken to the illusion of the prison world, then we are no longer at its mercy. It will no longer control us; we will have control over it. When we realise that this world is an illusion, we transcend its limitations and become co-creators of it.

* * *

Despite regular denials, Jung was given to frequent speculative excursions into metaphysics, but those speculations never seemed to have led him to believe that there was anything other than an objective physical reality to our world. He was very much grounded in the world and any world-as-illusion hypothesis was not something that would appear to have preoccupied him to any great extent, not in his public writings anyway. Nevertheless, he did explore the relationship between psyche and what we experience as physical reality, and nowhere more so than in his theoretical construct known as *synchronicity*.

Generally described as an "acausal connecting principle", the term synchronicity refers to the phenomenon of the *meaningful* coincidence—or near coincidence—of two events: one an event in the outside world, and the other an inner psychological state of mind. In Jung's view, when an inner psychological event, involving an unconscious image—coming into consciousness, either directly or indirectly via a dream image, an idea, or premonition—coincides with an outer situation with the same (or very similar) content, then a synchronicity is said to occur. Crucially, the events are not connected causally, but only through their shared, inherent meaning, without which the two events are merely coincidental. Synchronicity is predicated on a "psychically relative space-time continuum" linking psyche with the material world as two different, but inextricably related, aspects of the same fundamental thing, in which the non-psychic and the psychic can behave like one another without any causal connection between them (Sharp, 2010). Psyche and matter are one and the same thing, and their essence is energy. Although the inner and outer events of an instance of synchronicity might be phenomenologically distinct, their synchronicity is an expression, imbued with meaning, of their fundamental indivisibility.

The factor connecting psyche and matter is archetypal. At the heart of synchronistic events are the transcendent, unknowable—yet capable of being experienced indirectly—aspects of the archetypes, which Jung considers to be founded on a *psychoid* base. He describes (1962) psychoid as a soul-like, quasi-psychic, foundation that is only partially psychic, and quite possibly has an entirely different nature which he, tentatively, speculates might be spiritual. Although he had few, if any, qualms about making metaphysical assertions in writing that remained private during his lifetime—as *The Red Book* and the *Seven Sermons* attest—Jung was ever cautious about such statements in his public works. Nevertheless, in *Memories, Dreams, Reflections*, one of his final public works, he does suggest that we have good reason to suppose the existence of an uncomprehended absolute reality (ibid.). Synchronicity might then be considered to be the observation of an ordered wholeness within the collective psyche in which a particular instance of synchronicity is the dual expression of archetypal activity emanating from the psychoid dimension of the psyche. The two synchronistic events are expressions of a moment, and that moment is an archetypal fluctuation occurring within, and issuing from, the depths of the collective unconscious. Jung is positing a unified reality, an *unus mundus* (Latin for "one world"), underpinning all experience, yet he does not appear to suggest that physical phenomena are anything but real.

* * *

In *The Matrix* Morpheus instructs Neo that what he takes for reality is actually occurring inside a computer program, a "neuralinteractive" simulation which is the Matrix itself. Within the simulation, Neo's self-concept is not real either; it is merely a "residual self-image", a mental projection of a digitised identity. There are echoes here of Meister Eckhart, with a Gnostic twist. Eckhart claimed that when the Soul wants to experience something she throws out an image in front of herself and then steps into it. In the Gnostic tradition, the demiurge, accompanied by his archons, is the blind, ignorant, dark abyss of the shadow of the Soul. He wanted to create a world modelled on the image of the incorruptible, Pleromic harmony. However, he was ignorant (and arrogant) and lacked the true power of the Light of the Pleroma. The result was the corrupt, chaotic world into which we have been cast and held deluded into thinking is real. Similarly, the architects of the Matrix have projected a computer-generated dream world in which humanity is trapped. Until we realise our predicament, attain gnosis, and find a way out, we are nothing more than individual, virus-ridden, archon-controlled, software programs running within the operating system of the Matrix. Informed of his predicament, and in a tone that betrays his incredulity and difficulty in accepting the truth, Neo asks if the world he perceives is not, in fact, real. Morpheus responds rhetorically, "What is real? How do you define real?" Given his acosmic metaphysics (i.e., the universe is an illusion), it is no surprise that these same questions are ones that preoccupied PKD for most of his writing career. Indeed, these questions held an endless fascination for him and in his writing he would repeatedly revisit the theme of the true nature of our world, and whether the empirical or phenomenal world, which we generally consider as "reality", was, in any way, real. In his short stories and novels he frequently wrote about counterfeit worlds, alternative realities, and what he described as "pluriform pseudoworlds" (1977). PKD (2011) himself counts a total of twenty-one novels and short stories in which the theme of real vs. fake world featured.

In PKD's view, "... someone is causing us to see a universe that doesn't exist. Who is that someone? ... Satan [i.e., the demiurge]" (2008, p. 199). Elsewhere he stated that concealed beneath our ever-changing, phenomenal world, there was an eternal, unchanging, absolute reality (1978). He felt that this Black Iron Prison world, ruled by the Empire, is a counterfeit world superimposed over a deeper reality (2011, loc. 5688). However, to say that it is counterfeit is misleading, because there is no world actually there (loc. 6720). Reiterating the world-as-illusion theme in *The Divine Invasion* (2008), he describes this world, which he terms the lower realm, as the result of "transparent pictures permutating at immense velocity" (p. 65). In the novel, these pictures are archetypal forms from outer space which have been projected into the lower realm to become "reality". This idea of a world that is not substantively real, but only appears as such, echoes Einstein who claimed that, with regard to matter, we had all been wrong. What we consider to be matter (i.e., physical reality) is simply energy whose vibration has been lowered to the extent that it can be perceived by the senses. For Einstein, there is no matter; it has no objective reality. For PKD, our world is a mere phantasm, a fallen world, into which we have been thrown, enslaved by an evil entity that "projects data contoured to resemble a world" (2011, loc. 6720). Writing in his *Tractates*, PKD declares that the phenomenal world that we take for granted, and consider to be "reality", does not, in fact, exist. Its reality could not be confirmed and he considered it to be a hypostasis of information processed by the One Mind (i.e., the Pleroma) (2001). The essence of the universe is information. It is not three-dimensional, indeed, it is outside space and time altogether.

In other words, for PKD, this world is like *The Matrix*, and nothing more than the (mis-)interpretation of an underlying reality of which the essence is simply information.

However, despite his lifelong obsession with the quest to understand the nature of reality, PKD felt he never really got to the bottom of it. In a speech delivered in 1978, towards the end of his life, he acknowledges that he was unable to work it out. He recalls being asked by a student who wanted a pithy one-sentence definition of reality for a philosophy class paper, to which PKD could only respond with: "Reality is that which, when you stop believing in it, doesn't go away" (1978). After a lifetime devoted to exploring that topic he felt unable to define reality any more coherently. Yet, can there be a more accurate definition of reality? Nevertheless, he felt that as long as we are here, and continue to be deluded into thinking the BIP is real, we have to contend with it. With his inimitable wit PKD breaks off from an entry in his *Exegesis* one day by noting that he has to go as "a lot of publicans and sinners, tax collectors and other riffraff abound" (2011, loc. 1467), and, with some forbearance it would appear, he has to deal with them. Echoing the sentiment of Ellis, this delusional world is "real" for PKD—and us—as long as it lasts, and while we are here we have to deal with it, tax collectors and riff-raff and all. Render unto Caesar the things that are Caesar's and all that.

Regarding the concept of the world-as-illusion, PKD adds one fundamental insight that, depending on one's point of view, either enhances, or departs from, the metaphysics of the ancient Gnostics. For the Gnostics, this illusory prison world was purely the work of the archons. However, for PKD (2011), we humans are co-creators, along with the Empire—PKD's counterpart to the archons—in creating the BIP dream world. In his *Exegesis*, he claims that we are "forgetful cosmocrators" (loc. 15114) who have become imprisoned in a universe of our own making without realising it. Alternatively, he describes our illusory world as a mass hallucination, along with the opinion that we need to overcome the false notion that hallucination can only be personal (loc. 6899). In the *Tractates*, he states that we hypostatise the information we are fed into the phenomenal world (2001), although he does not mention the source from which we are fed this information. Elsewhere, he claims that "[W]e built this world, this space-time matrix" (ibid., p. 196). If this is so then, from the perspective of the Gnostic tradition, we are the archons since the archons created this world.

* * *

Within the domains of science and philosophy, the idea that our world is a holographic projection has been around since 1997 when it was first proposed by the physicist Juan Maldacena. However, although they might not have referred to it as such, the concept of the universe as a hologram, or otherwise illusory, has probably been known to mystics and wisdom traditions since time immemorial. For example, the idea of there being no inherent reality to the universe and that it is brought into existence by conscious observation extends back thousands of years to Vedic philosophy (Rosenblum & Kuttner, 2012, loc. 3239). One who subscribed to the holographic view of the universe was PKD, whose multifarious cosmogony includes a creator God who employs an artificial satellite he calls *VALIS* (Vast Active Living Intelligence System) to project a hologram which we mistakenly take to be reality (2008).

A hologram (from the Greek words *holos*, meaning "whole", and *gramma*, meaning "message"), is a three-dimensional image of an object encoded on a two-dimensional surface. Simple examples of unsophisticated and less than impressive holograms can be found in the security feature on a credit card or driving licence. The physics of holography is beyond the scope of this work, but simply stated, a hologram is, typically, created by splitting a laser beam into two identical beams. One beam, known as the object beam, is directed at the object, and the reflected light is redirected at the two-dimensional surface which will capture the hologram. The other beam, the reference beam, is directed onto the two-dimensional surface. It is the interference pattern resulting from the interaction of these two beams that is recorded onto the two-dimensional surface. Later, when the interference pattern on the two-dimensional surface is illuminated using a light source, a three-dimensional image of the object is produced. A hologram has some significant features. If a holographic image is viewed from different directions, it presents a three-dimensional image of the original object from different perspectives. Another fascinating property is that, unlike a normal image, for example, a photograph, which when cut in half yields only two separate pieces of the original image, a hologram, when cut in half, yields two holograms, each of which contains the whole of the original image. This holds true no matter how many pieces the hologram is cut into; the smallest piece of the hologram contains the entire image. Furthermore, if a piece of the original hologram is split, then each of its pieces also contain the whole of the original image.

In short, the theory that the universe is a hologram contends that the universe that we perceive is a three-dimensional image, in effect, an illusion, generated from information. Subscribing to this view, PKD asserts that what we mistake for reality is, in fact, the illusion of a projected hologram (2011, loc. 12926). He likens the Pleroma to a titanic hologram (loc. 7192). Similarly, in the *Tractates Cryptica Scriptura*, he states that the phenomenal world does not exist, but is, instead, simply "a hypostasis of the information processed by the Mind" (2001, p. 261). For PKD, the hermetic dictum, "as above, so below", refers to the idea that the universe is a hologram, but that the author lacked the term (pp. 257–258). In *Eugnostos the Blessed* of the Nag Hammadi Library it states that the Forefather "sees himself within himself as a mirror, and his image appears as Father by himself, Parent by himself, and reflection, because he reflects unconceived first existence" (Meyer, 2007, p. 277). Similarly, we might think that *Eugnostos* likens creation to be a mirror of the Pleroma because he lacked the word for a hologram. In his *Exegesis*, PKD states that his idea that the universe is a hologram is not original but is merely an updated description of the images flashed on the walls of Plato's cave. Like the prisoners in the cave who mistake the shadows cast on the cave wall for reality, we, likewise, mistake our holographic universe as being real. According to PKD, this holographic universe is a "spurious satanic interpolation … constituting a prison which shuts out information that … would reveal our *true* situation" (2011, loc. 6462, emphasis in original). In Gnostic terms, the fundamental nature of the fullness of the Pleroma is energetic information, and the archons have distorted this underlying information to project the illusory world in which we are imprisoned.

In PKD's view, our holographic universe is generated by the interaction of two hyper-universes in the same way that a regular hologram is created by the interference pattern of two laser beams (ibid., loc. 6480). In this holographic view—contrary to his earlier view that the Black Iron Prison and the Palm Tree Garden were two dipolar universes distinct from ours, one worse, one better—neither the Black Iron Prison nor the Palm Tree Garden is identical with our universe. Rather, he felt that our world is better considered as the holographic composite of the two, with each of them functioning as one of the two laser sources required to generate the hologram (loc. 6489). Rather than equating the Palm Tree Garden with the Pleroma, the superior upper world, and the Black Iron Prison with the universe, or the inferior created world, it would be more accurate to regard the PTG and the BIP as forming a pair of opposites within the fullness of the Pleroma, which, as *The Gospel of*

Philip suggests, are brothers which need to be reconciled and dissolved into one another in order to effect a return to the realm of light. This schema echoes the view of the Christian mystic Jacob Boehme who also believed in three worlds. First, the divine realm, an angelic paradise, and, second, an opposing dark world of fire and wrath. Both of these worlds are invisible, beyond the perception of the senses. The third is our world, which results from an eternal struggle between the two invisible worlds (Lachman, 2015).

The Gnostic idea of the world as an illusion, and PKD's notion of a holographic universe, finds an echo in the work of Kastrup (2011, 2015), who describes himself as a proponent of the philosophy known as monistic idealism (2011). Monistic idealism asserts that consciousness, rather than matter, is the ground of all being, much like Eckhart's concept of the Godhead. Well disposed to idealism was the British astrophysicist, Sir James Jeans (1877–1946), who felt that the material universe was a derivative of consciousness, rather than consciousness being a derivative of matter, and suggested that the universe should be regarded as a great thought rather than a great machine. Kastrup (2016) asserts that, given the latest findings in the field of quantum physics, the only worldview that can explain the experimental data is idealism, a view, he claims, which has been "presented symbolically in many creation myths from across cultures and history." The creation myth of the Gnostics—less the malevolence of the archons—would appear to be one of them. Opposed to what he describes as a "vicious, insidious stigmergy" (Kastrup, 2015, loc. 3279) aimed at the maintenance of the perspective of materialism, Kastrup's view is that consciousness is the only carrier of reality of which we can be certain (loc. 289). He claims all reality is excitations in the One Mind of consciousness, which he refers to as mind-at-large. Metaphorically, he describes the ground of all reality, mind-at-large, as a stream of transpersonal experiences in which our personal consciousness is simply a localisation, or a whirlpool, within the stream. (Personally, my whirlpool feels more like an emotional and mental maelstrom at times, so the analogy works for me.) All experience is the movement, or excitation, of water, and mind-at-large is the matrix in which whirlpools (individual consciousness), as localised patterns of water flow, consist of nothing but the stream's water (transpersonal consciousness) (loc. 338). This concept evokes the image of our individuality captured in the swirl pattern of our fingerprints. Our illusion of a personal identity, separated from the mind-at-large, is a result of this localisation (loc. 297). In an alternative analogy, Kastrup (2015) describes mind-at-large as suffering from dissociative identity disorder in which we are its "alters" (loc. 388). Dissociative identity disorder is a psychological condition in which a person has two or more distinct and persistent dissociated personalities, often referred to as alters (alternate personality). A person with this condition experiences an involuntary switching between alters, each of which has its own separate identity, characteristics, and behaviour. According to Kastrup, we are each an individual, dissociated personality within mind-at-large. In short, reality is grounded in a transpersonal dimension of consciousness in which we are what Kastrup describes as dissociated complexes, or alters (2015, loc. 436).

Kastrup (ibid.) maintains that, as an individual dissociated complex, we can only have a second-person perspective of an experience in mind-at-large. An original experience in mind-at-large, a ripple in the stream, reverberates within in an individual whirlpool (i.e., one of us), and our second-person perspective of the original experience is an amplification of the reverberation. These amplified, reverberating mental contents "end up obfuscating all other mental contents outside the whirlpool" (loc. 768). Like a TV set can only pick up the channel it is currently tuned into, an individual whirlpool only experiences the mind-at-large ripples that are currently reverberating within it in any given moment.

Kastrup (ibid.) goes on to explain consensus reality as "the shared second-person perspective of mental activity unfolding in a collective, obfuscated segment of consciousness" (loc. 419). Presumably, it is obfuscated only in terms of the first-person perspective. He claims that, since we all appear to share the same reality, the "particular storyline" being amplified by one whirlpool must always be the same as the storylines being amplified by all other whirlpools (loc. 964). He admits that exactly how this synchronisation happens "is an open question" (loc. 964), but it is by no means implausible given that all whirlpools are ultimately the same stream, mind-at-large. He describes this shared story (consensus reality), emerging from the obfuscated dimension of the collective psyche, as the dream of mind-at-large. Each one of us is a dissociated alter of mind-at-large partaking in the collective dream (loc. 2654): "Our individual psyches unite at a deep, obfuscated level, and the dream of consensus reality is imagined at that unified level" (loc. 2662). In an earlier work titled *Dreamed Up Reality: Diving into the Mind to Uncover the Astonishing Hidden Tale of Nature*, Kastrup (2011) also postulates that reality is the dream of what he refers to as the Source—which can reasonably be assumed to be identical with mind-at-large. He suggests that there is "… no distinction between the process of perceiving and the process of conceiving … its creation is a perception mirror of the Source's conception potential. Therefore, the idea of strong objectivity may be an illusion of our realm of reality" (loc. 1061). Patently, Kastrup, like the Gnostics and PKD, sees our world as a dream-like illusion.

There is, of course, also a clear parallel between Kastrup's (ibid.) view of a transpersonal form of consciousness, mind-at-large, in which we are individual, dissociated alters, and Jung's concept of the collective unconscious, which is the ground of individual consciousness, and from which our ego minds have become dissociated. The dissociated alters of mind-at-large (i.e., us) can also be likened to the Jungian concept of a *complex* within the individual psyche. In Jungian psychology, a complex is an emotionally charged cluster of ideas and/or images which accumulate around a particular archetype within the psyche. When a complex is constellated—activated due to some external situation—the result is an emotional response accompanied by physical symptoms or psychic disturbances. Invariably, complexes act with such a degree of autonomy that they can be considered as nodal points within the psyche, or splintered-off parts of the psyche that act according to their own will and laws, which, more often than not, is contrary to the habitual attitude of consciousness (Sharp, 2010). In the same way that a complex is a splintered-off part of the individual psyche, Kastrup's alter (or whirlpool) is a splintered-off part of the One Mind of consciousness. In other words, a complex is to the individual psyche what the alter is to One Mind. If that is so, then a complex is within an individual's psyche, which itself is a complex (alter) within One Mind; a complex within a complex.

Kastrup (2011) regards consciousness as a non-local field phenomenon in which the experiences of every conscious entity (whirlpool) within it "survive ad infinitum … as permanent experiences, or qualia" (loc. 345). (A qualia is an individual instance of subjective, conscious experience.) He also refers to thought patterns that form the underlying building blocks of everything ever experienced (loc. 1243). The correspondences with Jung's collective unconscious and the archetypes are obvious and one could argue that, in essence, Kastrup's mind-at-large is the collective unconscious, and his thought patterns are the archetypes. Indeed, he makes the connection that the collective unconscious is "somewhat related to the idea of a universal memory of qualia" (loc. 411). Quite clearly Kastrup's theories dovetail nicely with both those of Jung and PKD. Indeed, Kastrup's worldview would appear to sit somewhere between those of Jung and PKD, thus providing a perspective that helps to reconcile some of the differences between Jung and PKD.

A vociferous opponent of the materialist worldview, Kastrup (2016) claims that the latest experimental results in the field of quantum physics have demonstrated that the idea that there is a universe "out there", independent of our minds, is now untenable. Developments in quantum physics are increasingly giving support to the idea that there is no universe independent of consciousness, and that our world is an illusion or, at the very least, nowhere near as substantial as we have generally been led to believe.

Considered to date back to 1900, quantum theory now forms the theoretical basis of much of modern physics. Physicists Rosenblum and Kuttner (2012) note that quantum theory, coming after classical physics—which is now known to present a worldview that is fundamentally flawed—ought to be seen as encompassing classical physics, as a special case, rather than replacing it. Whereas classical physics does an adequate job of explaining the nature of objects larger than molecules, it is merely a very good approximation of their behaviour, and struggles to explain phenomena at the atomic and subatomic levels. In other words, classical physics only works satisfactorily in a finite band on the spectrum of existence. On the other hand, quantum theory perfectly explains quantum phenomena, but, so far at least, cannot explain the world of larger objects. This is perhaps due to limitations in the observing technology, rather any flaws in the theory (ibid.). Nevertheless, one third of the US economy is dependent on products based on quantum mechanics (loc. 98), with a great deal of modern technology now based on quantum principles (loc. 239), for example, lasers, transistors, and magnetic resonance imaging or MRI (loc. 1483). Furthermore, unlike its flawed predecessor, since its inception over a century ago, quantum theory has, so far, withstood the test of time. Rosenblum and Kuttner (2012) claim that it is the most "battle-tested" theory in science, with no predictions based on its principles ever having been demonstrated to be wrong (loc. 940). In short, as far as has been demonstrated to date, quantum theory is correct, whereas classical physics is an approximation only (loc. 533).

Quantum theory would appear to insist that the physical world that we experience is fundamentally dependent on our observation of it, and, most likely, our *conscious* observation of it. It appears to be leading to the inevitable conclusion that the act of observing an object to be in a particular place actually causes it to be there. Its existence becomes an actuality only upon its conscious observation, thus seemingly denying any physical reality to our world independent of our observation of it (loc. 260).

Quantum experiments have demonstrated that small particles—although, in theory, any objects—exhibit a wave-particle duality. Depending on the choice of experiment, a small object—for example, photon or atom—can be shown either: a) to exist as a particle at a particular location, or b) to appear as a waveform spread out over a large area, but not both simultaneously. Whereas the particle's waviness can be dispersed over an extremely wide area, when an observer looks in a given spot within that area, either the particle will be found there immediately, or it will not (loc. 1337). Thus, the act of observation of a waveform potentially converts an analogue phenomenon into a binary proposition in which, if the particle was found, caused something to come into existence. Extrapolating on this idea, we might consider the Pleroma to be analogue and the created world to be binary: the poles of the opposites within the Pleroma can oscillate instantaneously such that the male is not male, and the female is not female, whereas the created world, brought into existence through conscious observation, is binary in that it requires the tension between the differentiated opposites to spark creation into existence. Rosenblum and Kuttner (2012) stress that a potential particle's waviness in a particular area represents the probability of *finding* it in that location, and not the probability of it actually *being* there. It is the act of finding the particle in that spot, through observation, that actually causes it to be there. This, they say, is the tricky essence of what they refer to as the "quantum enigma" (loc. 1354). In quantum theory, it would appear that you can have your particle cake, and eat it too, just not at the same time. To some extent, it is not a case of wave *or* particle; it is a case of both wave *and* particle: the two states simply cannot be observed simultaneously. The ancient Gnostics would have loved quantum physics.

Rosenblum and Kuttner (2012) continue that whereas the act of observing a particle into existence in a particular location is a subjective experience for an observer, its quantum probability waviness, or wavefunction, is objective in that it is the same for everyone. Therefore, the quantum description for the phenomenon requires no particle in addition to the wavefunction of the particle such that the waveform of the particle is, objectively, synonymous with the particle itself (loc. 1381). There is no actual objectivity to the particle's existence (loc. 1765). Furthermore, the particle simultaneously "exists" everywhere covered by the waveform, until its observation in a particular location causes it to exist in that location (loc. 1892). Only the waveform, and not the particle, has any physical reality, objectively speaking (loc. 1765). Concentrating the waviness into a particular location, through conscious observation, causes the particle to come into existence (loc. 1785), but only for those observing. In short, the waveform is objective, the particle is subjective. A particle has no objective existence. In response to the well-known koan, "If a tree falls in the forest and there is no one there to hear it, does it make any sound?" quantum physics would appear to answer with a resounding, "No! Not unless there is a conscious observer." If there is no conscious observer, then not only does the falling tree not make any sound, there is no tree and no forest either. However, the Pleroma, PKD's One Mind, and Kastrup's mind-at-large can be regarded as conscious observers with an infinite capacity to dream anything into existence, independent of any *human* observers. So, does the falling tree make any sound? God heard it before it even existed. If—or perhaps, when—quantum principles scale up to larger objects, then there are no actual people either! We would exist only as human waveforms, and only come into existence when we are observed. Once again, extrapolating speculatively on this idea, perhaps we are waveforms in the collective unconscious, and only fall under the illusion of a separate self when we observe our particular waveform, or, in Kastrup's terminology, the act of observation of a particular ripple-set within mind-at-large brings a whirlpool into existence. The unconscious is, almost invariably, symbolised by water, and this seems all the more appropriate given quantum physics findings regarding the waveform nature of reality.

The fact that unobserved objects are mere probabilities and that nothing is actually real until it is observed into existence, raises the possibility that we live in a dream world. However, Rosenblum and Kuttner (2012) do not go this far, but, instead, maintain that observation creates an *objective* reality that is the same for everyone else (loc. 1809). However, this appears to equate "objective" with physical concreteness. A shared illusion, although not actually concrete, is, to some degree at least, objective. Quantum theory does not appear to preclude the idea that our perception of an objective concrete reality is, in fact, an illusion. We can speculate this from the findings of quantum physics, we simply cannot prove it … not yet anyway.

To date, quantum effects have only been demonstrated for small objects; however, if quantum theory holds for any size of object, then larger objects, houses, cars, people, do not actually exist until they are observed. Rosenblum and Kuttner (2012) contend that we never see this "… craziness with big things. For all practical purposes, big things are *always* being looked at" (loc. 2112). Really? Who is looking at the tree deep in the forest in the middle of the night? Does it cease to exist when the sun goes down and we cannot see it? Einstein, for one, did not like the idea that the moon might cease to exist when he was not looking at it (loc. 2323). The notion is, no doubt, disconcerting for most people. So, if large objects are continually being observed, who is the observer? It certainly is not human, not for all objects in our world. Perhaps the persistent illusion of our world is because One Mind, or the Pleroma—or the archons perhaps—or mind-at-large, is always observing it, or the computer that runs the Matrix is always online.

Rosenblum and Kuttner (2012) suggest that the implication of quantum theory that is perhaps the hardest to accept is the notion that not only does the act of observation create present reality, but it "also creates a past appropriate to that reality" (loc. 2302); in other words, the chain of events leading up to a given reality do not exist until that reality is observed into existence. The conclusion is that, through conscious observation, we are able to create a history "*backward in time*" (loc. 2302, emphasis in original). This lends some credence to PKD's claim that a great secret, known only by a few, including St. Paul, the Gnostic Simon Magus, Boehme, and Bruno, is the fact that "we are moving backward in time" (2001, p. 258). PKD appears increasingly percipient.

Another curious property of the quantum world is the principle of entanglement. Entanglement is the phenomenon in which, once entangled, particles remain connected to one another so that actions performed on one immediately affect the other, no matter the distance separating them: a phenomenon that so unsettled Einstein that he described it as spooky action at a distance. For example, if two particles are entangled, then when the polarisation of one twin is observed (thus causing it to have polarisation), the polarisation of the other twin is set immediately, regardless of the distance between the particles (Rosenblum & Kuttner, 2012, loc. 3453). Any two objects that have ever interacted with one another remain forever entangled, leading Rosenblum and Kuttner to conclude that there is a "mysterious universal connectedness" (loc. 2821) to our world that extends beyond the mere physical. At the psychological level, this connectedness might be none other than Jung's collective unconscious, and at the metaphysical, or spiritual, or Jung's psychoid level, this would correlate with the Pleroma that interpenetrates all that is.

Noting that quantum theory has implications far beyond what we consider to be the physical realm—the domain of science—Rosenblum and Kuttner caution against non-physicists incorporating quantum ideas to support their thinking in other domains, suggesting that those who do so be clear that their ideas are "merely suggested" (loc. 2861) by quantum physics, rather than being derived from it. Nevertheless—as far as this non-physicist is concerned—quantum theory does appear to be making less than subtle suggestions that our so-called reality is an illusion, and that consciousness alone brings this illusory reality into existence. Rosenblum and Kuttner note that there is no way to interpret the findings of quantum physics without encountering consciousness, but they acknowledge that, whereas most interpretations "accept the encounter [they] offer a rationale for avoiding a relationship" (loc. 2931). In other words, the world of science generally consigns what is often referred to as the "hard problem of consciousness" to the too-hard basket. In the meantime, we are dependent on the mystics and sages, indeed, the science fiction authors, of the world, unconstrained by the limits of science, to explore the nature of ultimate reality.

CHAPTER EIGHT

The seed and the sheaf

The kingdom of heaven is like to a grain of mustard seed, which a man took, and sowed in his field: Which indeed is the least of all seeds: but when it is grown, it is the greatest among herbs, and becometh a tree, so that the birds of the air come and lodge in the branches thereof.
—Matthew 13:31–32, KJV

A principal tenet of the Gnostic tradition is that the innermost core of every human being is a spark of the divine light. Our bodies and psyches might have been fashioned by the demiurge and his archons but our fundamental essence is a chip off the old block of the Pleroma. The canonical *Gospel of Luke* declares, "The kingdom of God is within you" (Luke 17:21, KJV). Similarly, the arguably Gnostic *Gospel of Thomas* contends that if the kingdom was in Heaven (i.e., in some transcendent realm "up there"), then the birds will get there before humans, and if it is to be found beneath the sea then the fish will be there first. Rather, the Kingdom of God is both inside as well as outside. Lachman (2015) succinctly captures the essence of the divine spark when he describes it as "our divine inheritance, some small part of the true God's emanation" (loc. 2360). In *The Gospel of Philip*, the divine spark is likened to a pearl which does not lose its value when covered in mud, nor increases in value when anointed with balsam. It remains forever precious in its owner's eyes; the essence of the divine spark is the Pleroma and each divine spark is intrinsically important to the Pleroma.

However, due to the error of Sophia, and the workings of the archons, this divine spark has become exiled in the material world. For the Gnostics, the divine spark has become imprisoned in matter. Renowned theoretical physicist Stephen Hawking described the human race as nothing more than a chemical scum on a medium-sized planet, orbiting an average star in an outer suburb of the universe. He considers humanity to be so insignificant that he doubts that the universe was created for our benefit. The Gnostics would tend to agree about the physical body, created by the archons, being a mere chemical scum, but where they would differ is that the physical scum that we are hosts a divine spark. And the created world, if not the entire universe, was not created for our benefit. It was created by the archons to farm humanity.

* * *

Jung's Gnostic vision has its version of the divine spark. Despite created beings having been differentiated out of the Pleroma, each being nevertheless contains the essence of the Pleroma within it. According to Jung, we are within the Pleroma, and the Pleroma is also within us, thus reflecting the maxim—common to most Western esoteric schools of thought, but most often associated with Hermeticism—that the infinity of the macrocosm is reflected within the finite of the microcosm. The quasi- (or reluctant) Gnostic poet William Blake (1757–1827) claimed that infinity was contained in a grain of sand, thus echoing the ancient Gnostics—not to mention Christ's teaching about the mustard seed, which Jung would reiterate in the *Seven Sermons*—that the entirety of the Pleroma resides within the smallest particle since both the infinite and the infinitesimal, as opposites, are contained within the Pleroma. Elsewhere, in his "Psychological Commentary on 'The Tibetan Book of the Dead'", Jung states that "the soul is assuredly not small, but the radiant Godhead itself" (1957a, p. 63). If we replace the term "soul"—often considered to be an individual's divine, innermost essence—with "divine spark", and note that Jung refers to the Godhead, as opposed to God, then he is, in effect, repeating his Gnostic assertion that the divine spark is, in essence, one and the same as the Pleroma. Jung continues that the "soul is the light of the Godhead, and the Godhead is the soul"

(p. 63). In the language of the Gnostics this would be "The divine spark is the light of the Pleroma, and the Pleroma is the divine spark." Jung also notes the divine spark's alienation from the Pleroma. In his "Psychological Commentary on 'The Tibetan Book of the Great Liberation'" (1954) he asserts that the trajectory of Western culture has resulted in a human mind that has become isolated from the primordial oneness of the universe to the extent that it is no longer the microcosm and image of the cosmic macrocosm. As a result, the factor in the psyche that acts as a mediator between the conscious mind and the unconscious has ceased to be the scintilla of the *anima mundi*, the World Soul. In other words, the ego has become alienated from the collective unconscious, the soul has been cut adrift from the Godhead, and, in Gnostic terms, the divine spark is estranged from the Pleroma.

* * *

The concept of the divine spark also features in PKD's Gnostic system. In the *Exegesis*, in a line that could have come straight from the Nag Hammadi Library, he declares that we are divine sparks enclosed in corruptible sheaves (2011). His view is that the "absolutely basic key" of the Gnostic tradition is "the encounter with the familiar in the midst of the alien landscape" (loc. 15428) in which the individual, as a partial self of the One Self, the One Mind, the Pleroma, recognises something that it has already seen, in other words, itself. The familiarity he is referring to is not the human ego's familiarity with the everyday world, it is nothing other than the divine spark remembering itself as both a part, and yet the whole, of the Pleroma. This is *the* gnosis of the Gnostics, and his assertion that it is the basic key of their philosophy would appear correct. Elsewhere in his *Exegesis* he references the microcosm-contains-the-macrocosm adage before adding that the spark is equal to the whole of the universal mind. He proceeds with the insight that the God within observes the God without, which is immediately reminiscent of the saying of Meister Eckhart that the eye with which he saw God was the same eye with which God saw him. PKD then notes that the spark and God commune with one another in a dialogue mediated through the body—a parallel with the ego-Self axis is clearly evident—and while the divine spark is communicating with God, continues PKD, "Satan is up at the McDonald's stand, ordering coweye burgers and plastic malts, thinking to keep his power" (loc. 1424).

In terms of his holographic view of the universe, PKD considers the divine spark within each one of us to be a fragment of the entire cosmic hologram, "intact gestalts but 'dimmer' or less defined" (loc. 5974). In the same way that a piece of a hologram contains the whole hologram, in a holographic view of the Pleroma, the divine spark, as a piece of the Pleroma, contains the entire Pleroma, only less so. If that sounds like a paradox it is because it is. As noted above, paradox appears to be the norm when grappling with the most profound mysteries. Elsewhere in the *Exegesis*, PKD claims that the piece of the hologram within us, the divine spark, is what is meant by the term the Logos, in other words, Christ. The divine spark is the indwelling Christ.

CHAPTER NINE

The self and the homoplasmate

I am come a light into the world, that whosoever believeth on me should not abide in darkness.

—John 12:46, KJV

Although direct inner experience of the divine is *the* imperative for salvation in the Gnostic tradition, gnosis, on its own, is not enough to ensure deliverance and a return to the Pleroma. Gnosis must be mediated in some way by an emissary, or saviour, from the transcendental realm of light, who descends from on high to rouse humanity from its somnambulistic imprisonment in the world of darkness. In Christianised forms of Gnostic thought, this emissary is, of course, Christ: "I am the light of the world: he that followeth me shall not walk in darkness, but shall have the light of life" (John 8:12, KJV). Similarly, in the Gnostic literature, Christ has been sent to bring light into the world. For example, in *The Secret Book of John*, the saviour is the light from the light—that is, *the* divine spark—who descends into the "midst of darkness and the bowels of the underworld" (Meyer, 2007, p. 131) to awaken humanity to its entrapment in the prison which is "the prison of the body" (p. 131). According to *The Gospel of Philip*, Christ came to correct the fall that occurred in the beginning,

85

that is, when Sophia erred and the demiurge and his minions created the material world. Prior to Christ's incarnation, those that came here did so from a realm they could not return to and found themselves in a place from which they could not leave, presumably meaning that those who came into this world from the Pleroma were unable to escape and, instead, became trapped in the world of matter. Then Christ came from the Pleroma bringing food from there and giving the light of life to all those who wanted it so that they would not die but could escape the world of darkness. In the words of St. Paul, "For in him dwelleth all the fullness of the Godhead bodily" (Colossians 2:9, KJV). In Gnostic terms, the fullness of the Pleroma is manifest in the divine spark of the realised Christ. The *Reality of the Rulers* teaches that the saviour comes into this world to reveal the spirit of truth. His mission is to teach humanity about everything, in other words, to impart gnosis, and to anoint people with the "oil of eternal life" (Meyer, 2007, p. 198). As a result, the anointed will be "… freed of blind thought. They will trample death, which is of the authorities. And they will ascend into the infinite light where this offspring is" (p. 198). The blind thought referred to is the delusion that mistakes this prison world of the archons for reality. The notion of "trampling" death is interesting and it may well be an echo of one of the sayings in *The Gospel of Thomas*. When asked by his disciples when he will appear to them, the saviour responds that "When you strip without being ashamed, and you take your clothes and put them under your feet like little children and trample them, then [you] will see the son of the living one" (Meyer, 2007, p. 144). Metaphorically, our clothes are the physical body and when we throw off the shackles of matter in the archonic prison world then we "trample" death, and can ascend to our true home in the realm of infinite light. The use of clothing imagery is a trope of Gnostic literature and its use appears in *The Gospel of Philip* where it teaches that the Gnostic must become clothed in the perfect light. The archons are unable to see those who wear the body of light and are no longer able to detain them in their worldly prison.

* * *

There is no saviour in Jung's *Seven Sermons*, however, there are some striking parallels between the saviour in the Gnostic tradition and one of the most significant components of Jung's psychology—arguably the central idea that underpins his entire work—the psychological postulate he referred to as the *Self*. In Jungian psychology, the Self is both the unifying and ordering centre of the whole psyche (i.e., including both the conscious and unconscious minds). In the same way that the ego is the centre of the conscious mind, the Self is the centre of the totality of the psyche. Jung described the Self as the centre of gravity of the psyche. In Jung's view, the realisation that we are far more than our egoic self, but are, in fact, our Self, was the goal of life. In other words, for Jung, Self-realisation was the ultimate purpose of the individual. Given that the Self encompasses both conscious and unconscious, it can only ever be experienced partially, either directly, to the extent that the Self is conscious, or else indirectly, by way of effect, or through symbols emerging from the unconscious. The unconscious component of the Self is considered to be the archetype of wholeness, which, as an archetype, is taken to reside in the collective unconscious. If, as Empedocles suggests, God is a circle whose centre is everywhere and whose circumference is nowhere, then, by analogy, the Self might be considered to be the centre of the psychic circle, and the collective unconscious its unbounded circumference. Yet, the illimitable locale of the Self is thought to extend beyond the unconscious (personal and collective) to a non-psychic (*psychoid*, see above) dimension of being, such that the Self is, ultimately, the objective wholeness beyond the psychic realm and therefore ineffable. The process of the realisation of the Self— which Jung termed *individuation*—involves the reconciliation and integration of all opposites within the psyche, principal among them the union of the conscious and unconscious psyches. However, this goal must be seen as a theoretical postulate that can never be fully actualised because, according to Jung, the opposites within the unconscious are forever generating further material to be reconciled and integrated. Consequently, in a pragmatic sense, the Self remains unknown and unknowable. However, the Self can, nonetheless, be experienced, to some extent at least, by the individual psyche. To the extent that the Self is beyond the psyche it can only act on the psyche indirectly and it does so by evoking the symbol-making function of the psyche, according to Jungian theory, and these symbols can, in turn, emerge into consciousness. Thus, it might be said that, in Jung's Gnostic system, the emissary is none other than a symbol of the Self that conveys its salvific gnosis into consciousness by way of the unconscious. Examples of symbols of the Self include Christ, the mandala, the cross, etcetera. Seen in this light then, rather than descending from the transcendent heights of the realm of light, Jung's Self can be considered the emissary from the unconscious depths. However, the emissary from above, and the Self from below, are one and the same. Ultimately, the Pleroma, and the collective unconscious are one. As a divine emissary, the Self is not only the cornerstone of Jung's psychology, it is equally central to his Gnostic vision.

In Jung's psychology the Self is considered to be a God-image, a symbolic representation of the inner conceptualisation of God, which is, simultaneously, the centre of the totality of consciousness (conscious and unconscious) as well as the union of all opposites within consciousness. In the Gnostic tradition, on the other hand, the God-image (i.e., the image of God) is not an image of the ineffable, ultimate Godhead (i.e., the Pleroma), which is not only beyond words but also beyond images. Rather, the image of God, in Christianised forms of Gnostic thought at least, is actually an emanation from the Pleroma which is, for all intents and purposes, the emissary, or the saviour, in other words, the Christ. Similarly, in Jung's Gnostic thought, the Self, in its positive aspects, is, more or less, one and the same as the Gnostic emissary.

For Jung, the archetype of the Self is exemplified by the figure of Christ. If we think in terms of a psycho-spiritual continuum, then the Self is the psychological aspect of the Christ, and the Christ is the spiritual aspect of the Self. They are one and the same thing at different dimensions of being. Nevertheless, crucial to understanding Jung's Gnostic Christ, or his reimaged Christ, is that it differs from the traditional Christian Christ in one very important aspect. In arguably his most scathing criticism of orthodox Christian theology he denounced their Christ as bereft of wholeness due to the fact that it embodied only the light and failed to incorporate anything that might be even remotely considered dark. Jungian thought, largely premised on his Gnostic vision, the *Seven Sermons*, is permeated by the coincidence of the opposites and his Gnostic Christ is no different. In sharp contrast to the traditional Christ figure who is wholly good, Jung's Christ also had to embody evil. Rejecting the Christian doctrine of *privatio boni* (the privation of good), which maintains that evil is insubstantial in itself and merely the absence of good, Jung, as was noted above, viewed evil as every bit as substantial, not to mention effective in the world and the human psyche, as good. The opposites are predicated on one another. There is no good without evil, no light without dark. Consequently, unlike the Christian Christ who has been stripped of evil which is now carried by his brother Lucifer, if there is to be any hope of a restoration of divine unity, Jung's gnosis demanded that his reconceptualised Christ embodies both good and evil. Jung reminded us that St. Paul understood the psycho-spiritual law which maintains that, "… when I would do good, evil is present with me" (Romans 7:21, KJV).

An insidious consequence, according to Jung, of the doctrine of *privatio boni*, coupled with a God-image that is wholly good, is that it leads to the proposition that all that is good comes from God while all that is evil is attributed to humanity—because, in the absence of any substance to evil, anything bad that is attributed to Lucifer, Satan, the Devil, is in name only. In Jung's view this unfairly encumbers humanity with the rejected darkness of the God-image in which, somewhat akin to the Gnostic emissary from the realm of light, Christ becomes the mediator between the opposite poles of a transcendent, wholly good God and a fallen humanity born in sin. However, rather than the bearer of the salvific gnosis, Christ, or the Self, becomes not only the mediator, but also the locus within the psycho-spiritual realm in which all opposites need

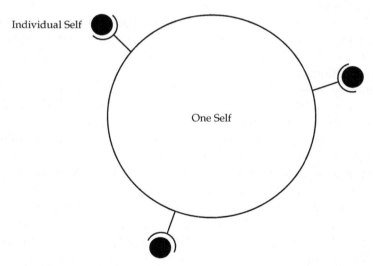

Individual Self

One Self

Figure 12. The One Self. An individual's Self is simply an aspect of the One Self.

to be reconciled, integrated, and ultimately transcended: conscious and unconscious, ego and Self, good and evil, light and dark.

One final point that ought to be made in this context relates to where the psychological predicate of the Self leads to—although this is rarely, if ever, mentioned in the Jungian corpus (as far as this author is aware)—and that is that there is, ultimately, only One Self. My Self is your Self; they are one and the same. We may experience that Self differently and have a wholly different relationship with it, but it is, nonetheless, the One Self. In this regard, the Self might be likened to a crystal with an innumerable number of facets. Each person's Self is but an individual facet of the crystal, the One Self. One Mind there is; One Self there is, and that One Self is the fullness of the Pleroma.

We might consider the individual Self to be a bit like a receptor site on the surface of a cell membrane in which the process of individuation, or Self-realisation, involves the ego, the extracellular molecule in our analogy, binding with the receptor site, the individual Self, on the surface of the cell, the one Self (Figure 12).

* * *

The concept of an emissary, or its equivalent, is also central to PKD's Gnostic system. In his *Exegesis* he acknowledges that he is rather taken by the idea of a "kind stranger God intruding into our screwed up chaotic world" (2011, loc. 4839). He was convinced that, due to a gross misperception as to the true nature of "reality", both as a species and as a planetary ecosystem, we are sick and in dire need of a "divine doctor-entity" (loc. 6279) to restore us. In the *Tractates Cryptica Scriptura* PKD refers to this spiritual physician, in other words, his Gnostic emissary, by the neologism *plasmate*, an immortal form of energy which he defines as living information and which he identifies with the Holy Spirit. Through a process he describes as cross-bonding, the plasmate can unite with a human being such that the human is permanently annexed to the plasmate, resulting in a further PKD neologism, a *homoplasmate*, a divine-human syzygy. This process was, in PKD's view, initiated by Christ, and can be regarded as the birth of the Spirit from above. Thus, like the Gnostics before him, but dissimilar to Jung, PKD's emissary comes from above. According to PKD, the plasmate, as a seed of living information, lay dormant for nearly two millennia in the buried codices of the Nag Hammadi Library and, for PKD, this is the true meaning of

Christ's parable of the mustard seed: the latent seed of gnosis, buried
for so long in Upper Egypt and discovered in 1945, can flourish into a
tree large enough for a new generation of Gnostic homoplasmates to
come home to roost in. PKD's concept of the homoplasmate—as well as
Jung's Self-realisation and the "docking" with the One Self—evokes the
words of St. Paul:

> I am crucified with Christ: nevertheless I live; yet not I, but Christ
> liveth in me: and the life which I now live in the flesh I live by the
> faith of the Son of God, who loved me, and gave himself for me.
> (Galatians 2:20, KJV)

A true Christian becomes a Christ, an individuated Jungian Gnostic realises the Self, and a Phil Dickian Gnostic becomes a homoplasmate.

PKD continues that in the act of cross-bonding an "interspecies sym-
biosis" occurs in which the plasmate, presumably male although not
stated as such, as an energetic form of living information, travels via the
optic nerve to the pineal gland in the human brain which it then uses
as a female host in which the union of the male and female polarities
produces an active form of the plasmate (2001, p. 260). It is through
this action of the plasmate, as an emissary from above, that VALIS,
PKD's counterpart to the Pleroma, transmits its gnosis.

PKD describes the plasmate as "mysterious as quicksilver" (2011,
loc. 8339), thus, either consciously or unconsciously, associating his
concept of the plasmate with the Roman god Mercury, and his Greek
counterpart, Hermes. Hermes is considered to be the messenger, or
emissary, of the gods, acting as the liaison between Heaven and Earth,
and the intermediary between the gods and humanity. Similarly, Jung
considered Hermes to be a symbol for the mediation between the conscious mind and the unconscious. Thus, for both PKD and Jung, the
Gnostic emissary is linked to Hermes.

Reminiscent of the words of *The Gospel of Matthew*, "Strait is the gate,
and narrow is the way, which leadeth unto life, and few there be that
find it" (Matthew 7:14, KJV), PKD expresses the sentiment that the path
to final redemption is a long, narrow, difficult one (2011), and that an
emissary from above, such as Christ, is an indispensable guide.

Without the emissary, we would wander blindly in the wilderness, and PKD continues that the process of reunion with the divine
is initiated by the emissary. Similarly, in the plot of *The Divine Invasion*

(2008), God has been driven off planet Earth which has now been taken over by the forces of darkness. An emissary, carrying God inside him, is needed to descend to Earth to restore divine order by awakening people to the fact that they are prisoners in a lower realm. The saviour is required "to burst the walls [of the prison], to tear down the metal gates, to break each chain" (p. 133). In PKD's Gnostic vision, Christ did not come as a sacrifice to atone for our sins; he came as the archetypal, immortal human to show us the way (back) to immortality. In terms of the holographic view of the Pleroma, the role of the saviour is first to give a practical demonstration of his presence, and second to eliminate the delusion that our world is real, but is, in fact, an illusion (2011, loc. 9324).

* * *

Two men have been in conflict which was, at times, quite violent, yet cartoonish. The conflict has been resolved and they are now friends. One of the men is now a government official, and the other is a renunciate who has adopted a simpler, contemplative, and sustainable lifestyle. The government official comes to the renunciate for help and, from his meditation cell, or cave, the renunciate advises him that his simple ways can provide food for the people when the systems of the world become stuck or break down. The renunciate seems to be my father, and, having visited my father while in town, I now go and visit my mother and sisters. My mother (in the dream) is an Indian woman. I embrace her, and she tells me she has a new car. She could choose from a range of colours, and she chose pink.

(Author's dream journal, January 2017)

One night, during the writing of this book, I requested a dream that would comment on the role of the Gnostic emissary. This dream is the unexpected result. Its content is largely personal material; however, if I attempt to interpret it in the context of this chapter's topic, then perhaps it provides some input that is relevant. The dream suggests that Spirit can only be received by withdrawing from the world, whether temporarily—for example, in a daily contemplative practice—or in a more ongoing lifestyle of renunciation. This contemplation of Spirit, from a place of withdrawal, provides the necessary spiritual nourishment to those in the modern world in which the systems are largely antithetical to the spiritual life. Spirit is not of this world. In the world,

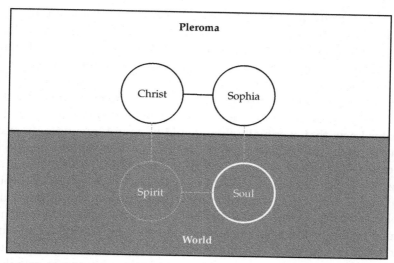

Figure 13. Spirit in the world but not of it.

but not of it. The dark-haired (Indian) woman with the pink (car) immediately makes me think of the dark-haired woman in PKD's 2-3-74 experience, whose fish pendant fired a beam of pink light at him. In PKD's Gnostic system, gnosis (i.e., salvific information) is transmitted to a person via a pink beam fired from *VALIS*, the vast active living intelligence system, which is, in effect, God. Thus, in PKD's view, the emissary, that is Christ, or Spirit, designated male in the Gnostic tradition, does not descend as such, but, rather, fires gnostic information from outside this world. In contrast, the soul, designated female, symbolised by the mother, Sophia, and her daughters, is very much in the world (Figure 13). The relationship between spirit and soul will be explored in more detail in the next chapter.

* * *

In one variant of PKD's vision he considers all of us to belong to the one cosmic entity, or God, and that we, as creator, created this fake world and then entered in it voluntarily. Unlike the Gnostic view that we were imprisoned here against our will, in this particular PKD vision, our descent into the prison world was an act of volition. Reminiscent of Plato's myth or Er in which reincarnating souls drink from the River Lethe (the River of Forgetfulness), leading them to forget their former selves in the next life, in PKD's vision we willingly forgot our identity, suffered in the world due to our amnesia, before coming across clues that had been placed deliberately by the creator in order to awaken us to the truth "when things got too rough—or, more profoundly, to set the limiting factor on this journey of calculated self-deception and imprisonment so it would have to end finally (whew—and just in time)" (2011, loc. 8395). These clues were left in an act of "cunning" in which the creator knew that eventually they would be found, reminding him of who he really is, that the created world is an illusion, and that he is imprisoned in it (loc. 8361). The reason the creator had for doing so was that he could permeate creation at all levels with divinity without realising that he was so doing (loc. 8449). Exactly why the creator would feel the need to do this, PKD does not adequately explain. In this particular metaphysical schema, we are one with God, we are the creator, and we are the archons, but, paradoxically, also the saviour, and the one who needs to be saved. *Salvador salvandus* (Latin for the saviour or that which is to be saved) as PKD liked to express it. When we realise our Christ nature, we are both the saviour and the saved; not two but one. "I and my Father are One" (John 10:30, KJV). PKD asserts this as one of his insights from years decoding his 2-3-74 experience: his investigation led him to realise that he is One with God. This is the gnosis of PKD. He claims that this is the highest realisation that a person can have: you are God (2011, loc. 8387). We are, or at least can be, too. We are, collectively, the One, and, individually, a microcosm of the One.

The idea of the creator bringing the world into existence and then entering into it in some way and being subject to its limitations, such that there are two aspects of the creator, unlimited outside creation, and limited inside creation, is not new. Kastrup (2016) cites a number of examples from world mythology of this same concept. For example, the Arandan, an indigenous Australian people, have a myth about a creator god, Karora, who dreams the world into existence while sleeping. He then wakes up inside his own dream and becomes subject to its constraints. During the subsequent night's sleep, Karora dreams further aspects of the world into being, before waking up, once again within the dream. Kastrup notes the alternation between two different states of consciousness: the dreaming state of unlimited ability to create, and a lucid dreaming state within the dream itself where Karora's powers are very much curtailed. Kastrup concludes from this myth—and others he cites— that: a) our universe is a mental creation (e.g., a dream, an illusion, or a thought, depending on the particular myth), and b) having imagined the universe into existence, the creator then enters the universe. What these myths teach is that rather than the universe being considered to be "out there", independent of mind, it ought to be recognised as being in the mind of God as a product of divine imagination. As such, the universe can be seen as the dream of God, which he enters in order to experience his own creation. Living creatures are nothing other than God's myriad penetrations into creation (ibid.). As a divine spark of the Pleroma, the microcosm of the macrocosm, humans do this every night. During deepest sleep we are one with the creator outside the dream, and then we "wake up" into the dream world of consensual "reality". According to Comella (2014), the renowned mythologist, Joseph Campbell (1904–1987) subscribed to this view, referring to life as one great dream of a single dreamer in which the dream characters (us) also dream (loc. 1001).

* * *

If we were to superimpose the emissary in both Jung's and PKD's Gnostic schemes, highlighting their relationship to the upper realm of the Godhead (Pleroma)/VALIS (One Mind), and the created world where the human ego finds itself, it might yield the following (Figure 14):

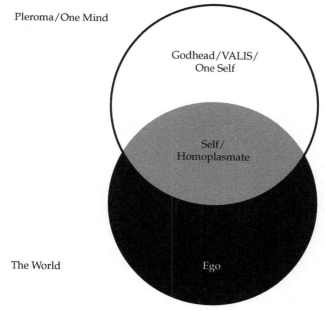

Figure 14. Jung's and PKD's Gnostic emissaries superimposed.

In the same way that there is really only One Self in Jung's system, PKD declares at the end of his *Tractates* that, despite the myriad names we might have for it, there is only one Immortal who comes as an emissary and we are that being.

CHAPTER TEN

The virgin and the whore

Little Alice fell down the hOle, bumped her head and bruised her soul
—Lewis Carroll, *Alice in Wonderland*

Discussions involving the terms "spirit" and "soul" can be ambiguous and inconsistent—often unnecessarily so. Where one commentator uses "spirit", another uses "soul" to mean, or so it would appear, the very same thing. Others use the terms, which are rarely defined, interchangeably, as if they are synonymous. For example, the *Oxford English Dictionary*, which really ought to know better, defines "soul" as the spiritual part of a human being! No doubt much of the confusion is due to the ineffable nature of what the terms are being used to articulate. In many instances, however, their interchangeable use is simply literary laziness. This distinction between spirit and soul was fundamentally important to the Gnostics and greater clarity is required.

If any generalisations can be made amid the confusion then the soul is, more often than not, taken to mean the animating factor in a human (or animal) that is unique to each person, and defines his, or her, individual essence. On the other hand, spirit is typically the element, or perhaps the medium, through which the person is linked to the divine. Wilderness guide, ecotherapist, and depth psychologist with a Jungian influence, Bill Plotkin has provided a helpful discourse on the subject, including definitions for "spirit" and "soul" that have considerable utility for any discussion on these loaded terms. Plotkin (2003) defines soul as "the vital, mysterious, and wild core of our individual selves, an essence unique to each person, qualities found in layers of the self much deeper that our personalities" (p. 25). Soul is the essence of each person. It is personal in nature and constitutes a person's individuality and all that is unique about that person. At the very core of our being, our soul is our most intrinsic self, our true self, in distinction to the person we typically identify with and present to the world. In contrast, Plotkin defines spirit as "the single, great, and eternal mystery that per-meates and animates everything in the universe and yet transcends all" (p. 25). Unlike soul, spirit is impersonal and common to all people, and forms the matrix of our collective cosmic citizenship. If the soul is an entity with being-ness, then spirit is that being-ness. Often thought to come from "up there", spirit is equally to be found within. It is both transcendent and immanent. It contains all, yet pervades all. If spirit sounds a lot like the Pleroma it is because it *is* a lot like the Pleroma; the Pleroma is known as the Great Invisible Spirit. Continuing with the spirit/soul distinction, Plotkin notes that, "[S]oul embraces and calls us toward what is most unique in us. Spirit encompasses and draws us toward what is most universal and shared" (p. 25). In terms of a crude (very crude) analogy, we might liken our soul to our individual TV set and spirit to the same TV channel that we can all tune into. In short, one spirit, many souls, where, as Plotkin puts it, "each soul exists as an agent for spirit" (p. 25).

Whereas there are a number of points of correspondence between the Gnostics' view on spirit and soul, and the generalisations given above, there are some notable differences which will be explored in this chapter.

* * *

Author of a number of books on the subject of Gnosticism, including a work dedicated to *Gnostic Writings on the Soul*, Andrew Philip Smith defines the soul, from a Gnostic perspective, as the "quintessential human element, poised between the material and the divine, between body and spirit" (2008, p. 27), thus positing a tripartite model consisting of body, soul, and spirit which is typical, not only of Gnostic systems,

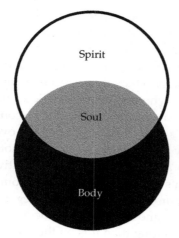

Figure 15. The tripartite nature of the human being: spirit, soul, and body. The spirit is of the Pleroma, the body is of matter, and the soul is what links them.

but also prevalent in both Western philosophy and Christian mysticism (Figure 15). For example, in the words of St. Paul, "And the very God of peace sanctify you wholly; and I pray God your whole spirit and soul and body be preserved" (1 Thessalonians 5:23, KJV).

The spirit is wholly of the Pleroma, indeed, insofar as the Pleroma interpenetrates the created world, the spirit, as it vivifies all beings, is in effect identical with the Pleroma. The body, on the other hand, is wholly of the world of matter. The soul, existing at the intersection of spirit and body, but having a fundamentally different nature to both, can nevertheless interface to both and therefore function as the intermediary between them. In the context of spirit being our connection to the divine, in the Gnostic tradition, the spirit, or perhaps more accurately, the quantum of spirit that resides in, and vivifies, the human being, is identical with the divine spark. "The Spirit itself beareth witness with our spirit, that we are the children of God" (Romans 8:16, KJV).

Some Gnostic systems considered there to be three categories of people corresponding to these three components of human being: the *hylic* (from the Greek work *hyle*, meaning "matter"), the psychic (from the Greek word *psyche*, meaning "soul"), and the pneumatic (from the Greek word *pneuma*, meaning "spirit"). Smith rightly suggests that, rather than viewing these three types of people as forming some kind of caste system, even if it did operate as such, an individual person's categorisation depends on which aspect of the tripartite nature that person is focused on. The hylic is rooted in physicality and the world of sense perceptions, the psychic adds awareness and engagement with psychological process, whereas the pneumatic's chief concerns are spiritual. However, these categorisations need to be considered fluid in two ways. First, a person's focus evolves, hopefully, over the course of life from a predominately hylic existence—which is nothing better than the life of an animal—to an increasingly greater cultivation of a spiritual life. Second, a person's focus can, and, indeed, out of necessity, has to shift from moment to moment (Smith, 2008). Regardless of the extent to which one has attained gnosis, a person's focus is going to be far more pneumatic when meditating than it is on the rather more hylic activity of putting the garbage out. After moments of gnosis, which are no doubt relatively brief in duration, even the most pneumatic of Gnostics must return to the mundane chores of chopping wood and carrying water.

In *The Reality of the Rulers*, the archons created the first human body from the soil of the earth. Later, the demiurge blows into the human giving him a soul. However, with only an archonic soul and an earthly body, the human is lifeless and it is only when the Spirit descends from the "adamantine land", in other words, the Pleroma, and takes up residence within the human does he becomes a living soul. The soul might animate the body, but the soul needs spirit to vivify it. Without spirit, the soul is a lifeless soul.

The Reality of the Rulers continues that the archons came to the first human, Adam, and they "cut open his side … like a living woman" (Meyer, 2007, p. 192) before repairing his side with flesh in what was her place. As a result, Adam lacks spirit and is now endowed only with soul. This suggests that the spiritual side, called Eve, of the originally androgynous Adam has been removed, thus resulting in Adam as mere soul, and spiritual Eve. It would be both simplistic and erroneous at this point to assume that this particular Gnostic text is designating soul as male and spirit as female. Something more subtle is being presented here: when the twin poles (male/female) of the original androgynous unity are split apart and manifest in matter they lose their spiritual nature and are reduced to a lower level of existence, the archonic, animal soul level. The myth has simply been told from the male point of view—its author was undoubtedly a man. If it had been told from a woman's perspective then it may well have postulated an original Eve who loses her spiritual essence when her androgynous nature is split in two as a result of Adam being removed from her side.

Subsequently, Eve, the woman of spirit, comes to Adam who declares, "You [Eve] have given me life. You will be called the Mother of the living" (Meyer, 2007, p. 193). The (re)union of spirit and soul, the restoration of the primal syzygy, generates life. Without reunion both twins of the syzygy are lacking their spiritual essence, they are mere souls, and nothing more than the living dead. This is the crux of Gnostic soteriology.

On the Origin of the World also teaches that the first human, Adam, was fashioned by the archons with both body and soul, but without spirit, and therefore lacking true life. He was a "lifeless vessel, since [he] was formed like an aborted foetus, with no spirit" (Meyer, 2007, p. 213). On the fortieth day, Sophia blows her breath into Adam and this brings him to life. However, he can only crawl along the ground and is unable to stand up. Smith (2008) notes that Adam's inability to stand up symbolically means that, lacking in spirit and having only a soul, which is considered to be a lower level of existence to spirit, he is unable to raise himself above the level of matter. Sophia then sends her daughter Zoe (which in Greek means "life"), who, in her earthly incarnation, is called Eve. Eve has come to instruct Adam on how to raise himself so that "the children he would engender might be vessels of light" (p. 214). Eve tells Adam to live and get up off the ground. Immediately, on her command, Adam stands up, opens his eyes, and—as in *The Reality of the Rulers*—he addresses her as the "Mother of the living" who has given him life.

In the corpus of Gnostic literature that forms the Nag Hammadi Library the only text that deals exclusively with the journey of the soul is, as its name suggests, *The Exegesis on the Soul*. Its teachings are couched in heavy sexual imagery—particularly sexual promiscuity—and in keeping with this theme, Scopello (2007) notes in her introduction to the text that the three key moments of the soul's life are: a) its original virginity, followed by b) its prostitution on Earth, and finally, c) its redemption and return to the Pleroma.

The text states that while the soul, which it designates as female, was alone with the Father, she was a virgin and androgynous in form. In other words, as long as the purity of the primal syzygy (female soul, male Father) was intact, the soul remained whole and in the Pleroma. However, for reasons unstated, the soul fell down into a physical body and entered human existence. In the Gnostic tradition, the fall is not being born in sin, it is the rupture of the male and the female unity. Consequently, the soul, having lost her pure state, is plunged into the material world where she falls into the midst of thieves, shameless men who violate her by raping her or seducing her with gifts. Now defiled, devoid of her original purity, she gives herself as a whore to everyone who would abuse her. She yields to them as if they were her master. In return, she receives nothing from her abusers "except the filth they left when they had sex with her" (Meyer, 2007, p. 227). The offspring who result from her promiscuity "… are mute, blind, and sickly. They are disturbed" (p. 227). It should be noted that the powerful sexual imagery is purely allegorical and not to be taken literally. Indeed, *The Exegesis on the Soul* is clear that it is discussing the prostitution of the mind and not the prostitution of the body. Barnstone and Meyer (2003) remind us of the words of St. Paul which have been quoted above but are worth repeating here, "For we wrestle not against flesh and blood, but against principalities, against powers, against the rulers of the darkness of this world [i.e., the archons], against spiritual wickedness in high places" (Ephesians 6:12, KJV). In a similar vein, *The Apocryphon of James* states that the body cannot sin without the soul. Whereas the spirit can save the soul, the body can kill the soul; however, it is the soul's attachment to the body that is the cause of death. So, in effect, the materially addicted soul kills itself. Unlike some puritanical elements of Christianity, the Gnostics had no aversion to the body *per se*. It was not the body that could be corrupted, or was liable to sin, but the soul.

Returning to *The Exegesis on the Soul*, the soul's act of giving herself (willingly) to all those that would defile her, and becoming servile to them, means the soul has been seduced by the distractions of the material world. Materialism, physicality, and the pleasures of the senses have become her masters and she their slave. Addicted to the passions of the psyche and the flesh, she is trapped in the world of shadows. For the Gnostics the baubles of the material world are snares which bind the soul to the fetters of matter. Nothing that glitters in this world is gold. In order to be saved, the soul needs to reject her "former whoring and … having sex with whomever she desires" (p. 230), and only once she has "cleansed herself of the pollution of adulterers" will she be rejuvenated as a living soul. However, the soul is powerless to conceive by herself. Like Sophia without her male counterpart, the soul is unable to conceive on her own and needs her male counterpart. Being only one twin of a pair of opposites, the soul is unable to engender life. Her polar opposite is required and so her consort is sent down from the Pleroma into the whoredom of the realm of matter to rescue the fallen soul who is imprisoned by the archons. Her saviour is referred to as the "bridegroom" and the soul is now referred to as the "bride", symbolically pointing to the union of spirit and soul that is so crucial to Gnostic soteriology. This mystical marriage occurs in what is referred to as the "bridal chamber". *The Gospel of Philip* notes that animals, slaves, and defiled women cannot enter the bridal chamber: it is reserved for free men and virgins. If we can see past the inherent sexism, there is a deep esoteric teaching in this statement. Animal souls who are enslaved by their addictions to the distractions of the world, and who prostitute themselves to them, bar themselves from the rite of the mystical marriage. Only those who have freed themselves from the bonds of physicality and attained the purity of the living spirit can enter the bridal chamber.

The bridegroom is not only the bride's betrothed but also her older brother which, according to Smith (2008), is an esoteric indication that the reunion of spirit and soul is a new experience and, at the same time, a recovery of the soul's lost birthright. The virgin becomes a whore, before returning to her former purity in the Pleroma. Smith suggests that this mystical wedding of spirit and soul in the bridal chamber is the goal of the Gnostic and that such a union is the fulfilment of gnosis. I would go further, and suggest that the ultimate goal of the Gnostic is the return to the Pleroma and that the union of spirit and soul is the means of its attainment. According to the *Exegesis on the Soul*, the reunion of the spirit with the soul in the bridal chamber is the true resurrection from the dead, deliverance from the control of the archons, liberation from the world of corruption, and the way back to the Pleroma.

It should be made clear here that it is the soul, and not the person, that is female. The soul is female regardless of the gender of the fleshy garment hosting it. That said, however, the nature of the opposites is that they only have meaning in relationship to one another. If we designate soul as female then it implicitly means that it is female in relation to something else that is, relatively speaking, male. In this case, the soul is female in relation to the spirit which is correspondingly designated male.

According to Scopello (2007), the soul in *The Exegesis on the Soul* represents every Gnostic, man or woman, who reads the text and sees their own life story reflected symbolically in the myth. The earthly sojourn of the Gnostic soul is, metaphorically speaking, one from an original virginity, through a descent into prostitution, before a return to virginity. It is one of the idyllic bliss of ignorance in the Pleroma, before a fall into matter and the pain of ignorance in the world of shadows, and then a return to the bliss of gnosis when restored to the Pleroma. This return journey of the soul evokes the idea of being reborn and is reminiscent of Christ's words to Nicodemus:

> Jesus … said … "Except a man be born again, he cannot see the kingdom of God." Nicodemus saith unto him, "How can a man be born when he is old? Can he enter the second time into his mother's womb, and be born?" Jesus answered … "Except a man be born of water and of the Spirit, he cannot enter into the kingdom of God. That which is born of the flesh is flesh; and that which is born of the Spirit is spirit." (John 3:3–6, KJV)

There could be multiple, equally valid, interpretations to this esoteric teaching, and one possible explanation is that the water referred to is the water which reflected, *ennoia*, the first thought of the divine thinker, the first image of God which, if God is designated male, is his female counterpart. In other words, anyone born of water and Spirit, and who lives as spirit rather than at the level of matter, is the divine child of the Mother-Father.

In the Gnostic tradition the soul clearly has a dual nature: the divine aspect, or the living soul, that comes from the Pleroma, and the material aspect, or animal soul, that comes from the archons. The soul is not considered to be inherently "lower" than spirit, it is simply that in its animal state it exists at a lower level of existence and its task is to elevate itself to the level of spirit, reunite with it, and thus effect a return to the Pleroma. *The Reality of the Rulers* notes that the archons are weak and that what is only of soul has no power over spirit. Therefore the animal soul, bestowed on humans by the archons, cannot grasp what is of spirit. The text continues that the archons are from below, but the image of incorruptibility—which the archons tried, and failed, to replicate as the animal soul—is from above. The *Authoritative Discourse* is particularly blunt in regard to the fallen state of the soul. It states that when the soul, originally in a state described as the spiritual soul, was cast into a body, it became the sibling of lust, hatred, and envy, in other words, it fell to the level of the material soul. The body came from lust, and lust came from material substance. Even if as little as a lustful thought enters the mind of a pure soul then that soul has already lost its purity and become contaminated. This is a clear echo of the Christian maxim that "whosoever looketh on a woman to lust after her hath committed adultery with her already in his heart" (Matthew 5:28, KJV). The *Discourse* continues that having left the gnosis of the Pleroma behind, the soul became an animal in the world and fell into a life of bestiality.

If a male/female pair of opposites is to be made out of spirit and soul then it must be made very clear which soul, or which aspect of the soul, is being paired with spirit. Only the living soul, that descended from the adamantine land, or resulted from Sophia blowing life into the first human, is the female counterpart of the male spirit. It is this soul, and this soul alone, which unites with the spirit in the bridal chamber. The animal soul that the first human received from the archons is not the spirit's counterpart and does not form part of the union with spirit.

A variation on the theme of the dual nature of the soul occurs in *The Revelation of Peter* which makes a distinction between mortal souls and immortal souls. The mortal soul is condemned to death, forever enslaved, and destined for eternal destruction since it is created "to serve its own desires" (Meyer, 2007, p. 493). On the other hand, immortal souls are different. Until their time has come, they may resemble mortal souls, but once their true nature is revealed they will turn their back on the ways of the mortal soul and "alone", in other words restored to unity, will realise their immortality. The mortal soul is the animal soul of the archons that remains as such, the immortal soul is the living soul from above that chooses reunion with spirit and a return to the immortal realm of the Pleroma. When the animal soul raises itself up to be a living soul then soul and spirit can be viewed as the two sides of the one coin, one transcendent, the other immanent, somewhat akin to a Möbius strip in which the two surfaces become a single continuous surface.

The Gnostic soul has a choice. According to Smith (2008) the soul must choose between the two poles of its existence. In what he describes as a tug of war between spirit and body, the soul can completely identify with the body, or it can seek permanent union with its spiritual counterpart in the bridal chamber. In other words, the soul can either lose itself in the material world, giving itself over to the passions of the mind and of the flesh, or it can seek its redemption, its reunion with spirit, and a return to the Pleroma. *The Gospel of Thomas* is both direct and succinct: "Woe to the soul that depends on the flesh" (Meyer, 2007, p. 153). Noting that figs are not gathered from thistles, or grapes from thornbushes, *The Apocalypse of Peter* teaches that evil cannot produce good fruit. In similar fashion, only the living soul can lead to salvation, whereas the animal soul leads to perdition. As long as the soul persists with her promiscuous gallivanting she "will suffer what she deserves" (ibid., p. 229). Those souls that fail to reunite with spirit but remain rooted in the world of matter become, according to Smith (2008) their "own petty demiurges" (p. 55). Like the creator of this world before them, the demiurge along with his archons, earth-bound souls create their own personal worlds from a place of both ignorance and arrogance, oblivious of the light above.

Another analogy used in the Gnostic literature to describe the soul's journey is to state that it is sick while in the world of matter. For example, the *Authoritative Discourse* discusses how the sickness of blindness wounds the soul's eyes. Symbolically, being blind means to have fallen foul of the deep sleep imposed on humanity by the archons and to be in a state of ignorance, in other words, lacking gnosis. The corollary, of course, is that gnosis, spiritual insight, is required to remedy the blindness and restore health, or spiritual wholeness. In the *Authoritative Discourse* the cure for blindness is administered when the bridegroom anoints the eyes of the soul with his healing balm. This is a clear echo of Christ's healing of the blind man that is recounted in the canonical Gospels.

> "As long as I am in the world, I am the light of the world." When he had thus spoken, he spat on the ground, and made clay of the spittle, and he anointed the eyes of the blind man with the clay, and said unto him, "Go, wash in the pool ..." ... He went ... and washed, and came seeing. The neighbours ... said they unto him, "How were thine eyes opened?" He answered and said, "A man that is called Jesus made clay, and anointed mine eyes, and said unto me, 'Go to the pool ... and wash,' and I went and washed, and I received sight." (John 9:5–11, KJV)

The man has been blind from birth, which, symbolically, means he was born into the ignorance of deep sleep imposed on humans by the archons. From the Gnostic perspective, Christ, the saviour, is the emissary from the Pleroma who has come with the light of gnosis and to dispel the darkness of ignorance. The spirit restores insight, in other words, gnosis, to the fallen soul.

Another interesting point made by Smith (2008) regarding Gnostic teachings on the soul is that they establish a link between cosmology and psychology in a way that suggests that,

> Gnostic cosmology and psychology are identical in purpose, or at least interlocking. Cosmology describes the universe from an external perspective, psychology from an internal viewpoint. *Essentially there is no difference between the two.* Just as the world of matter is furthest away from the true God and the Pleroma, so the body is the furthest away from spirit and the Pleroma. (p. 55, emphasis added)

As a transpersonal psychologist, I concur with Smith in collapsing, or, indeed, removing, the gap between Gnostic cosmology—which here can be viewed to include both its metaphysics and its spirituality—and psychology. As previously noted, there are various ways of defining transpersonal psychology, and one that is particularly apt is that transpersonal psychology acts as the bridge between psychology and spirituality (Rowan, 2005). Late in life Jung (1962) speculated that the archetypes, and by extension, the matrix in which they exist, the collective unconscious, were founded on a partly psychic, partly spiritual substrate. Some theological critics of Jung accused him of attempting to psychologise spirituality as if in doing so he was, in some way, reducing spirituality. It is not a case of psychology over here, and spirituality over there, and never the twain shall meet. What Jung's critics, and those who separate psychology and spirituality as two completely distinct domains, fail to realise is that spirituality and depth psychology are different dimensions on the one psycho-spiritual continuum (or, alternatively perhaps, different perspectives on the same thing, two sides of the same coin). Whenever a Gnostic encounters an either/ or proposition, invariably she should be looking for the inherent both/and. The collective unconscious is not merely the psychological counterpart of the Pleroma, it *is* the Pleroma, albeit at different levels of being. Phenomenologically they may appear and function differently, but their essence is identical.

* * *

In Jungian psychology, spirit and soul appear, in the guise of their psychological counterparts, in Jung's theory of the anima/animus. Jung postulated the anima and animus as the contra-sexual elements within the psyche; the anima (from the Latin word for "soul"), is the inner, typically unconscious, feminine aspect of a man's psyche, and, correspondingly, the animus (from the Latin word for "spirit"), is the inner, unconscious, masculine aspect of a woman's psyche. The anima and animus are collective (i.e., archetypal) rather than personal factors; in other words, the anima is the archetypal image of the unconscious feminine in man, and the animus if the archetypal image of the unconscious masculine in woman.

The key to understanding the anima/animus theory is that it is premised on what Jung considered to be a fundamental law of the psyche: its self-regulation. In the same sense that the body is forever seeking homeostasis, Jung believed that the psyche also seeks to maintain its equilibrium through the compensating effect of the unconscious. If the ego adopts a position that is too one-sided this will result in the activation of the unconscious which responds with psychic content (e.g., dream images or, in cases of more acute imbalances, symptoms of neuroses), which provides a counter-position to compensate for the imbalance of the conscious attitude. Jung's anima/animus theory sticks to the narrative of a self-regulating psyche and sees a man's feminine anima compensating for his masculine ego, and a woman's masculine animus compensating for her conscious feminine identity. Anything that is excluded from the conscious identity tends to accumulate in the unconscious according to Jung; therefore, a man who exclusively identifies with his masculinity will repress his feminine traits which will then comingle to form his inner image of the archetypal anima. Similarly, a woman who identifies only with her femininity at the expense of her masculine side will repress that masculine side, of which the various aspects will form her inner animus figure.

An important aspect of the anima/animus is its function as the interface to the inner world of unconscious processes, both those that are evoked from our engagement with the outer world, as well as those that emerge from the unconscious itself. As such, the anima/animus can be thought of as occupying a location between a person's conscious mind and the collective unconscious, where it acts as a bridge between the outer and inner worlds, and facilitates a dialogue between the ego and the Self, the image of God within the unconscious. In short, the anima/animus is the doorway into the depths of the psyche (Stein, 1998). In *The Matrix*, not only does Trinity complete the Holy Trinity of Father (Morpheus), Son (Neo), and Holy Spirit (Trinity), she also symbolises the anima. She introduces Neo, as his twin, Thomas A. Anderson, to Morpheus, an encounter which ultimately leads Neo to transform into the One. In other words, Trinity-as-anima mediates the dialogue between Thomas A. Anderson, Neo's ego, and the unconscious, symbolised by Morpheus, the god of dreams and, by extension, the unconscious. Through his confrontation with the unconscious, and all that Morpheus reveals to him, Neo realises his Self and becomes the One.

However, it ought to borne in mind that the anima/animus theory is a psychological model, and a model, by definition, is a simplified description that seeks to elucidate something far more complex. Models can sometimes be overly simplified and just a bit too "tidy" and, while facilitating understanding on the one hand, they can fail to capture the rich intricacies of the phenomena being described on the other. The messy business of life more often than not simply cannot be pigeonholed into a neat model. This would appear to be the case in Jung's anima/animus theory which, with its all too black-and-white gender stereotyping, completely misses the mark with regard to acknowledging the nuanced shades of grey of gender identity that we are far more aware of today. In reaction to this, there seems to be a trend today to regard the anima as the female aspect of the personality, and the animus the male aspect, regardless of the gender of the individual. Alternatively, the anima is simply considered to be the inner part of the personality in contrast to what Jung termed the *persona*, and what might be considered the outer part of the personality. However, this smacks of political correctness and completely ignores the self-regulation of the psyche and the compensating influence of the unconscious on the conscious mind that is central to Jung's psychology. A far more useful revision of the anima/animus theory is offered by pre-eminent Jungian Murray Stein (1998) who summarises the anima/animus theory in a way that both honours the underlying principles of Jungian psychology, and yet moves past Jung's rigid gender designations. Stein proposes that the essential feature is that the relationship between the ego and the anima/animus archetype within the unconscious is characterised by the male/female polarity of the self-regulating psyche. To the extent that the ego identifies with the masculine pole, the anima/animus adopts a compensatory feminine nature, and, similarly, to the extent that the ego identifies as feminine, the anima/animus will appear masculine.

Jung's anima/animus theory is preconfigured in the *Seven Sermons* in the sermons which provide a discourse on the dual themes of spirituality and sexuality. Although these psycho-spiritual powers might not immediately appear to be polar opposites in the same way that, for example, light and dark, and up and down, clearly are, Jung believed that spirituality and sexuality did, indeed, form a pair of opposites. However, they are not just *a* pair of opposites, but from a human perspective, *the* essential pair of opposites. In Jung's view, as was noted above, the world comes into being through the differentiation of opposites in which the tension between the differentiated poles generates the necessary energy potential that gives rise to creation. Specifically, it is only through the interplay of the cosmic forces of spirituality and sexuality that humanity can come into being. Furthermore, in Jung's Gnostic system, it is *only* within humanity that the interaction between spirituality, symbolised by a bird, and sexuality, symbolised by a serpent, can occur, hence the figure of Abraxas, who was introduced above and who epitomises the clash of opposites, displays the bird-human-serpent symbolism (Figure 10).

In the *Seven Sermons*, Jung's discourse on these themes begins with a spirituality that is characterised as celestial, and a sexuality characterised as earthly. However, contrary to the more common gender attributions that designate Heaven as male and Earth as female, Jung presents a celestial mother and an earthly father. Although not without precedent in ancient mythology, this assignment does seem conspicuous. Jung identifies sexuality as a daimon which he describes as a "half human soul", having an earthly nature and associated with the dead. Its counterpart is the daimon of spirituality, another half human soul, which comes from above and, presumably, by inference, is associated with the living. Both these halves, spirituality and sexuality, are required to form a whole and where they meet is in the human soul. Jung asserts that the sexuality of a man is more earthly and descends, whereas that of a woman is more spiritual and ascends. In contrast, the spirituality of a man is more heavenly and is oriented upwards towards the infinite, whereas the spirituality of a woman is more earthly and is oriented towards the finite.

Hoeller (2002b), who has provided a detailed analysis of the *Seven Sermons*, notes the deeply esoteric nature of the work and cautions against any facile interpretation of the text that might attempt to equate spirituality with the masculine principle and sexuality with the feminine principle. In contrast to the more familiar characterisations of the male and female principles, the *Seven Sermons* attributes the masculine with qualities more normally associated with the feminine, and vice versa. Hoeller concludes that both the celestial mother and the earthly father have a direct influence on the male and female spirituality, and an indirect influence on male and female sexuality. The celestial mother governs female spirituality and male sexuality, whereas the earthly father governs male spirituality and female sexuality. In other words, the male and female principles are both dual-natured and, within each pole of the male/female polarity, there exists a spirituality/sexuality polarity with different but complementary governing principles. This immediately evokes the Taoist yin/yang symbol in which both sides of the syzygy contain the seed of its opposite (Figure 16). This interplay of the primal syzygy is so crucial to the Gnostic tradition—and, therefore, the thesis of this book—that the Taoist symbol is displayed in each chapter heading. This polarity within a polarity serves to illustrate the dynamic nature of the opposites in the Pleroma in which the twin poles within any given syzygy have not been differentiated. Perhaps somewhat akin to an alternating voltage in electrical systems in which the voltage reverses direction periodically, the twin poles within the syzygy can switch their polarity, one moment male, female the next, and vice versa.

Any rigid assertions of these male/female categorisations might be seen as a little discomfiting and, as Jung did regarding his anima/animus theory, Hoeller rightly advises against being too dogmatic on

Figure 16. The polarity within polarity of male and female spirituality and sexuality.

these matters. It should be noted that Jung's Gnostic vision—as well as Hoeller's analysis—on the subject of the spirituality/sexuality and male/female polarities are discussions on metaphysical principles, and not about individual men and women per se. The male and female polarities are *a priori* psycho-spiritual dynamics, or daimons, that existed prior to differentiation out of the Pleroma, and long before the archons fashioned male and female bodies. How these dynamics manifest in a flesh-and-blood human is subject to the myriad variations of human existence.

* * *

In a variation of PKD's Gnostic cosmology, when the unity of the Godhead was split in two, and the "primordial fall" took place, the terrible male spirit "side that arouses fear and trembling" remained in the transcendent realm, and the kind and compassionate, immanent, female, or soul, side fell into the created world where she "debased herself" (2008, p. 223). Having been separated for millennia, the male (spirit), and female (soul) halves of the Godhead need to be reunited to restore the primordial unity. In his *Exegesis*, he contrasts the fall of the soul, and the reunion of the soul with spirit, as two births. The first is the birth into a human body in the Black Iron Prison, an event over which we had no control, but which happened to us. The second birth, or rebirth, is crucial, according to PKD, and must be initiated by an act of volition. It is something which must be accomplished by one's own effort, but, at the same time, cannot be done without spirit. Like the bride preparing the bridal chamber for her beloved in *The Exegesis on the Soul*, those seeking the second birth must find a way to entice, welcome, and attract spirit. PKD notes that two agents are required to fulfil the second birth: water and spirit. In the chemical reaction that is the mystical marriage in the bridal chamber, the bride is the water and the bridegroom is the spirit. In PKD's gnosis, the water element is activated through the sacrament of baptism; however, we are unable to obtain spirit on our own: "We must wait for it to arrive, having done our part, the water part" (2011, loc. 1217). Paraphrasing the Greek philosopher Plotinus (204–270 CE):

> We ought not to question whence it [the spirit] comes; there is no whence, no coming or going in place; it either appears or does not appear. We must not run after it, but we must fit ourselves for the

[spirit] and then wait tranquilly for it as the eye waits on the rising
of the Sun which in its own time appears above the horizon and
gives itself to our sight. (The Six Enneads, V.8)

Elsewhere in the *Exegesis*, PKD concurs with Meister Eckhart in that the
human soul is the image of God and, out of this image, God can be recon-
stituted as "the original reborn from its image" (loc. 3971). Rendered in
the concepts of the ancient Gnostics, the human soul, expressing itself
as the living soul, in union with spirit, manifests the image of God
within the human. This corresponds with the aim of Jung's psychology
in which the realisation of the Self also manifests as the image of God.
For Jung, the Self and the God-image (distinct from God itself) were one
and the same thing.

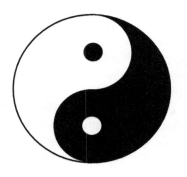

CHAPTER ELEVEN

Slavery and freedom

Ye shall know the truth, and the truth shall make you free.

—John 8:32, KJV

The only goal of the Gnostic is to return to the Pleroma. For the Gnostic, salvation is the liberation of the divine spark from the spatio-temporal, material prison world, and its reinstatement to the realm of light, or into the depth and silence. Whereas the Neoplatonist might seek a return to the One, the Gnostic seeks a return to the Zero, in other words, the Nothingness of the Pleroma. In the text known as *On the Origin of the World* it is stated that the light will overcome the darkness and that the darkness will be dissolved, before adding that everyone must return to the place where they came from. That is, everyone must leave the world of darkness and return to the source of the light and eternal rest in the depth and silence of the Pleroma. *The Gospel of Philip* notes that when the bride and bridegroom come together in the mystical marriage there is only one name for their union and that is rest; the rest that results from nothing but the pure contemplation of the divine. As the saviour said, "Come unto me, all ye that labour and are heavy laden, and I will give you rest" (Matthew 11:28, KJV). Or, in the words of Meister Eckhart,

115

God is at home and it is we who have gone out for a walk. Gnostic salvation requires an end to our wandering in the valley of death and our homecoming to rest in the Pleroma.

The various texts of the Nag Hammadi Library highlight various aspects of this return journey. Paramount among these is, of course, the need for gnosis, the *sine qua non* of Gnostic salvation and the return to the Pleroma. *The Gospel of Philip* teaches that ignorance, the antithesis of gnosis, is the mother of all evil and leads to death. Citing John 8:32, "Ye shall know the truth, and the truth shall make you free" (KJV), *Philip* adds that ignorance is slavery, and gnosis is liberation. If a person knows the truth, she will find the fruit of that truth, and if she joins with that truth, it will bring fulfilment, in other words, a return to the Pleroma. Salvation is often referred to as the resurrection in the Gnostic texts and in his introduction to *The Treatise on Resurrection*, Thomassen (2007) notes that the resurrection and return to the original purity of the Pleroma, dependent on salvific gnosis, includes the realisation that our spiritual essence is something that we already possess. It is not something that we need to develop, it is something we need to realise. In this regard, Gnostic salvation is somewhat akin to the Dzogchen tradition in Tibetan Buddhism in which liberation involves awakening to one's true nature. In the case of the Gnostic, the true nature is that one's spiritual essence is the divine spark. One is already of the Pleroma, in the Pleroma, and permeated by the Pleroma. Seen in this light, the resurrection is anamnesis of our divine heritage rather than an event. Upon this realisation, the attainment of gnosis or enlightenment, one realises, for the first time, one's perfection. The Gnostic returns to the Pleroma transformed, or, in the words of the poet T. S. Eliot, after a peregrination through the material realm, one returns to the Pleroma with gnosis as if for the first time. Essential to this realisation is, amongst other things, the awareness that the spatio-temporal nature of our so-called reality is merely part of the archons' deception. Nevertheless, according to Thomassen, in the case of the Gnostic, more than this awakening is required. The soul, as a potential Christ, must incarnate and attain the resurrection, as a necessary precondition for the restoration of the original perfection in the Pleroma. As such, there is "both an 'already' and a 'not yet'" (ibid., p. 51) aspect to Gnostic salvation. The "already" part is the perfection of the indwelling divine spark. On the other hand, the "not yet" part demands the efforts of the Gnostic, and *The Treatise on Resurrection* informs us that, although we already have the resurrection, we carry on in our earth-bound zombie state as if we will die, without realising that the mortal part of us is as good as dead already. The text makes it clear that everyone must practise ways to escape from this prison world, otherwise they will continue to be led astray and kept in ignorance. Blind faith in the saviour is not enough. Receptivity to the spirit, and the salvific gnosis that is brings, coupled with one's own efforts are required to attain liberation.

In order to achieve salvation, or the resurrection, and the return to the Pleroma the Gnostic texts teach that one must first escape from the prison of matter imposed on humanity by the archon slave masters. *The Teachings of Silvanus* implores the reader to which it is addressed to prepare to escape the archon-controlled world of darkness by turning his back on the things of the world in which there is no profit. Instead, he must purify his outer life in order that he may be able to purify his inner life. Similarly, *The Dialogue of the Saviour*—which some would argue is not truly a Gnostic text—recounts, as the name suggests, a supposed dialogue between the disciple Matthew and the saviour. Matthew asks why we do not go to our rest at once. In other words, why do we not return to the Pleroma immediately? The saviour replies that we will rest only when we leave behind what cannot accompany us (i.e., the physical body) and all that burdens us. For the Gnostics, the resurrection is not a bodily one, but the reverse, an escape from all that is material. Similarly, *The First Revelation of James* states that we will not be saved until we "throw off blind thought, this bond of flesh surrounding [us]" (Meyer, 2007, p. 325). Taking an equally dim view of the human body, *The First Revelation of James* views the crucifixion as esoteric symbolism rather than as a historical event, and speaking from the perspective of the Christ within rather than as the earthly human, states that the saviour did not suffer. He, as Christ, was neither distressed nor harmed; rather, the crucifixion was "inflicted upon a figure of the rulers, and it was fitting that this figure should be [destroyed] by them" (p. 327). The saviour continues that the flesh is weak and it will get what has been ordained for it. The biblical aphorism, "Render therefore unto Caesar the things which are Caesar's; and unto God the things that are God's" (Matthew 22:21, KJV) comes to mind once more. Caesar is a symbol of the demiurge, the emperor of the Empire, who presides over the Black Iron Prison. The body belongs to the archons and returns to the dark lords of matter, the spirit belongs to the Pleroma. The soul is crucified between spirit and matter, and must choose the way in which it will go. *The Gospel of Philip* states that as long as what it refers to as the root of wickedness is hidden it remains strong. However, when it is recognised, it will be dissolved. It only has power over us because we have not recognised it. The root of wickedness is the deceit of the archons, and they only have power over us because we have not seen through the veils of deception and realised our imprisonment in matter. This would later find an echo in Jung who taught that we do not attain gnosis by imagining beings of light, but only by making the darkness conscious, an endeavour that is so disagreeable that it is generally eschewed. For anyone making a reasonable analysis of the Gnostic literature, there can be no shadow of a doubt that the Gnostic pastors of antiquity considered this world to be a corrupt, fallen place and they wanted to get the flock out of here. At the end of *The Matrix*, Neo claims that despite our desire to change the world the Matrix will remain our cage. We cannot change the cage; nevertheless, it can become our chrysalis in which we are transformed; but to be liberated we have to change ourselves. The Black Iron Prison can simply imprison us, or it can rehabilitate us. The prison is not going to change, or at least, not until we do. Echoing the reputed words of Gandhi, we need to be the change. Jung's view was the change had to begin with the individual: it does not happen "out there", it happens "in here".

According to the *Authoritative Discourse*, the choice of life or death is offered to everyone and each must choose for himself or herself. In regard to this choice, Meyer (2007) refers his reader to a number of similar passages of canonical scripture including the following: "Verily, verily, I say unto you, he that heareth my word, and believeth on him that sent me, hath everlasting life, and shall not come into condemnation; but is passed from death unto life" (John 5:24, KJV). In Gnostic terms, whoever receives the saviour's gift of gnosis and applies that knowledge to attain liberation crosses from death to life. Later in *The Gospel of John* Christ declares,

> Verily, verily, I say unto you, I am the door of the sheep. All that ever came before me are thieves and robbers: but the sheep did not hear them. I am the door: by me if any man enter in, he shall be saved, and shall go in and out, and find pasture. The thief cometh not, but for to steal, and to kill, and to destroy: I am come that they might have life, and that they might have it more abundantly. (John 10:7–10, KJV)

To the Gnostic, this passage states that the realised Christ opens the door to the Pleroma for the Gnostic faithful. The thieves and the robbers are the deceptions of the archons who keep us enslaved and obscure the way back to the Pleroma. The archons come to steal, kill, and destroy. Likewise, in *The Wisdom of Jesus Christ*, the saviour comes to free the immortal human from the bondage of the robbers. As Morpheus says in *The Matrix*, humanity will never be free as long as the Matrix, that is, the illusory, archon prison world, is in existence. The red pill or the blue pill? In *The Exegesis on the Soul*, the first step in making the choice, and the beginning of salvation, is repentance from the animal soul's "former whoring". Salvation is achieved when the soul reunites with spirit and consummates the mystical marriage in the bridal chamber. This is the resurrection from the dead, freedom from captivity in the world of matter, and the return to the Pleroma. *The Exegesis on the Soul* also makes reference to Luke 14:26—which states that if one does not hate one's own life, one cannot be a disciple of the saviour—and notes that one must, not only hate one's own life, but must hate one's own soul in order to follow the saviour. The soul being referred to is the animal soul of the archons, not the living soul from the Pleroma. The Gnostic must forsake this earthly life of captivity and "hate" his, or her, animal soul.

Regarding the fate of the human soul the Gnostics believed that not all souls will be saved. For example, the interlocutor in *The Secret Book of John* asks if all souls will be saved and returned to the Pleroma. The saviour responds that only those on whom the Spirit of Life descends can be saved. Without the Spirit of Life an individual cannot even stand up which, symbolically, as Smith (2008) has pointed out, suggests that the soul is unable to raise itself above the material plain of existence. In the Gnostic tradition the descent of Spirit on its own is not enough; the soul must play its part and only those who have received the Spirit, and who reject the wickedness and corruption of this world, "expunge evil" from themselves, and avoid being led astray by the counterfeit spirit of the archons, will inherit eternal life. On the other hand, those souls in whom the counterfeit spirit has grown strong will be burdened by the fetters of matter once more, cast back into the wickedness of the world and blinded once more by the veil of deception spun by the archons. At the time of physical death when these souls leave the body they will be given over to the archons, bound in chains, and immured once more in the Black Iron Prison. Espousing the concept of reincarnation,

The Secret Book of John teaches that the cycle of rebirth into this world continues until the soul attains the gnosis that lifts the veil of deception and, through its efforts, realises perfection and is saved, returning to a state of eternal repose in the Pleroma. The Gnostic tradition affirms the doctrine of reincarnation, and it appears in a number of places in the Gnostic literature; however, it does not appear to be something the Gnostic should be overly concerned with. The task of the Gnostic is to escape from the material world, and return to the Pleroma, whilst in this present incarnation. The interlocutor, John, then asks about the fate of those souls who have achieved true knowledge but have then turned away from it. Reminiscent of the teaching that those who blaspheme against the Holy Spirit will never be forgiven, but are in danger of eternal damnation (*The Gospel of Mark*, 3:29, KJV), the saviour answers that they will be ushered to a place where the "angles of misery go" (Meyer, 2007, p. 129) and where repentance is impossible. There, they will be held until "those who have blasphemed against the spirit will be tortured and punished eternally" (p. 129). In similar vein, *The Gospel of Philip* teaches that people who have been enslaved against their will can be freed; however, those who have been freed by their master and then sell their souls back into slavery can never be freed again. On the other hand, regarding the fate of the divine spark, the spirit within us, it will return to the Pleroma. In truth, it never really left, because it *is* the Pleroma. It is merely the archons' veil of deception that gives us the illusion that we are not from the Pleroma, and are separated from it. God is at home, it is we who have gone out for a walk … and got lost in Dante's dark wood along the way.

Another feature of Gnostic soteriology is the idea that it involves an ascent through a series of planes in order to reach the transcendent realm of light. These planes are thought to be controlled by the archons and the aspiring Gnostic must carefully navigate a way past the archons who will do what they can to thwart the Gnostic's efforts and keep him, or her, enslaved in the lower realms. In the Gnostic tradition, the Pleroma is considered "higher", and the fallen world of the archons "lower". However, the "ascent" ought to be seen as metaphorical, and is not to be thought of as a movement upwards. It should be considered as an expansion of consciousness and an increase in gnosis. Turner (2001) identifies two patterns of soteriology in the Gnostic texts attributed to the Sethian sect. The first, which he refers to as the descent pattern, involves the saviour who descends from the Pleroma with gnosis.

This intercession from above by the saviour has been discussed in a previous chapter. The second, the ascent pattern, is described by Turner as gnosis attained by contemplative ascent. The first requires the Gnostic to become receptive to the saviour and to receive gnosis as a gift through grace. The second need to be worked for and attained through the Gnostic's own efforts. The texts which elaborate on the theme of the ascent pattern present salvation as a contemplative journey involving a visionary ascent through a series of inner planes. The process is one of self-realisation in which the way of ascent is the reverse of the original descent from the source. It entails an undoing of the process of emanation out of the Pleroma, and culminates in a return to, and a dissolution in, the highest transcendent realm. Typically, these inner planes correspond to the planets, each of which is characterised by the unique challenges it represents to the Gnostic aspirant. These challenges are nothing but the archons' attempts to keep the Gnostic soul trapped in the world of shadows. Turner suggests that these visionary ascents are not necessarily one-off events in which gnosis is acquired in the mother-of-all mystical experiences—but let's not rule that out—rather, he considers them to be brief events during the life of the Gnostic, which provide a foretaste of the ultimate ascent the soul will make following the death of the body. This idea is captured eloquently by the French writer and poet, René Daumal (1908–1944):

> You cannot stay on the summit forever; you have to come down again. So why bother in the first place? Just this: What is above knows what is below, but what is below does not know what is above. One climbs, one sees. One descends, one sees no longer, but one has seen. There is an art of conducting oneself in the lower regions by the memory of what one saw higher up. When one can no longer see, one can at least still know. (2017)

Like one of those computer games that has multiple, increasingly difficult levels where it takes many attempts and many hours of practice to reach the higher levels, the attainment of gnosis is, no doubt, a process of incremental gains over a lifetime of dedicated practice. After each partial trip up the mountain to render unto God what is God's, the Gnostic practitioner returns, with a little more gnosis, to the world and, out of necessity due to the limits of the body, to the task of rendering unto Caesar while preparing for the next attempt at the summit. In the words of the Buddhists: before enlightenment, chop wood and carry water; after enlightenment, chop wood and carry water.

A crucial component of Gnostic soteriology, and one that would have a particularly profound influence on both Jung's gnosis and his psychology, is the need to both a) reconcile the opposites, and b) in the case of the Gnostics, realise the ultimate dissolution of the opposites in the Pleroma. *The Gospel of Thomas* teaches that if one is whole then one will be filled with light, but if one is divided, then one will be filled with darkness. In other words, when one has integrated the opposites, when the bride and bridegroom have consummated their mystical marriage in the bridal chamber, then one will be filled with the light of the Pleroma. On the other hand, as long as the opposites are differentiated, and the bride has forsaken her betrothed and continues whoring, one remains condemned to the darkness of the world. These are fundamental distinctions in the Gnostic tradition: the Pleroma is characterised by light and wholeness; this world is characterised by division and darkness. *The Wisdom of Jesus Christ* speaks of the need to be united with spirit such that two become one as it was in the beginning. *The Gospel of Thomas* elaborates further on the theme and claims that one will only return to the Pleroma when the two are made into one, when the inner is made like the outer, and the outer like the inner, when upper and lower are reconciled, and when the male and the female are reunited into a single being so that their gender differentiation is dissolved. Then, and only then, will the Gnostic see the light of the Pleroma. Meyer (2007) notes the close correspondence to the following passage from canonical scripture:

> For as many of you as have been baptized into Christ have put on Christ. There is neither Jew nor Greek, there is neither bond nor free, there is neither male nor female: for ye are all one in Christ Jesus. (Galatians 3:27–28, KJV)

The balancing, and ultimate dissolution, of the male/female polarity is also captured by the Indian mystic Ramakrishna (1836–1886). In reference to Brahman, the ultimate male divinity in Hinduism, and Shakti, the creative power of the divine feminine, Ramakrishna is said to have proclaimed that Brahman is Shakti, and Shakti is Brahman. They are not to be considered distinct but two aspects, one male, and one female, of the same Absolute. The *Tripartite Tractate* also states that the return to the primal unity of the Pleroma is premised on the balancing of the opposites. The return, like the beginning, is unitary where there is neither male nor female, neither slavery nor freedom, neither immortal being nor mortal being. All that will exist is the perfect balance of the opposites such that they cancel one another out which, in this particular text, is symbolised by the figure of Christ. The description of the Pleroma as a state of rest has already been noted, and this state includes all syzygies in a perfect state of harmonious equipoise, no movement, no vibration, no sound, just silence. As Eckhart expressed it, there is nothing so much like God in all the universe as silence. Elsewhere Eckhart described the quiet mind that contemplates the Godhead as one on which nothing weighs, one free from worries and the ties that bind it to the world, free from all self-seeking, but wholly merged with the Godhead and dead to any notion of a separate self.

* * *

A WWII radio operator is in discussion with his German counterpart. "We" (presumably, the British) seem to be holding the German's brother as a POW. When I realise this, I take over the conversation with the German radio operator and arrange a prisoner swap, one of ours being held captive by them in exchange for his brother. The exchange takes place on neutral ground between our respective sides' front lines. At the end of the exchange I want to meet and shake hands with the German radio operator. I tell him that when the war is over and peace is restored I will meet him in Germany and we will play chess, drink beer together, and watch the sunset.

(Author's dream journal, November 2016)

This dream largely speaks for itself and little commentary is required. It is clearly a reiteration of the passage from *The Gospel of Philip* that teaches that light and darkness, and life and death, and left and right, are siblings which cannot be separated. Consequently, good is not good, evil is not evil, life is not life, and death is not death. Each pair comprises the complementary poles of an underlying unity which have become differentiated. Ultimately, symbolically representing by the setting sun, each pair of opposites will dissolve back into unity. This concept of sibling polar opposites dissolving into unity is symbolised by the German radio operator and his brother being reunited. Elsewhere *The Gospel of Philip* makes it clear that when Adam and Eve were conjoined there was no death. Only when they were separated did death come into being, and only when they reunite will death cease to be. In other words, only when the primal syzygy differentiated into its opposing poles on the plane of matter, when the male and female split, did death come. Paradoxically, as is the way with the opposites, not only did the differentiation of the opposites create the energy potential essential for life, that same differentiation also instituted death. Life and death are siblings, which, in characteristic fashion, the Gnostics have flipped on their heads: to be born into this world is death; to escape this world and return to the Pleroma is life.

The dream also symbolises the way in which opposites are reconciled within the psyche according to Jungian psychology. Given his view that the psyche is a self-regulating system forever seeking psychic equilibrium, Jung believed that any exaggerated conscious attitude is compensated by an equal and opposite unconscious counter-position. As opposites, the conscious and unconscious attitudes are the two poles of an underlying unity, and their reconciliation and integration involves elevating consciousness to a level that transcends the separation of the poles and realises their inherent unity. According to Jung, this is achieved through a dialectic exchange (symbolised by the communication with the German radio operator) between the ego (i.e., the conscious attitude) and the unconscious counter-position, in which both positions are given due regard and any notion of right/wrong valuation is suspended. The two opposing positions will generate what Jung describes as an energy tension within the psyche. If the person can hold this tension of the opposites during the ongoing dialogue between conscious and unconscious attitudes, a third position, embodying the inherent unity of the opposites, will emerge that transcends the two opposites. This third position becomes the new conscious attitude to which the unconscious, once more seeking compensatory balance, responds with a further counter-position. The dialectical exchange begins anew and repeats *ad infinitum*, presumably, or until the person has achieved the idealised, but practically unattainable, goal of complete psychic integration. This process, as well as the resultant third position, Jung termed the "transcendent function" (1957b), and the method he developed to achieve it was active imagination (see above). The dream is suggesting that the opposite positions in the archetypal battle of good vs. evil, symbolised by the British at war with the Nazis, need to be transcended, and a higher level of consciousness attained that recognises their underlying unity in which good is not good, and evil is not evil. Furthermore, the chess symbolism reframes the clash of the light and the dark, symbolised by the white and black pieces, as a game. This is bitter medicine, and it is difficult to come to terms with it in the face of the horrors that unfold daily on prison Earth. Perhaps when good and evil have been dissolved, and duality has been transcended, we can look down from a place of higher consciousness, and see the struggle of the light and the dark within human experience as a game. This is hard to do from the perspective of a pawn within the game. However, in PKD's view, we are the archons, and the archons are us, and when the war is over, hopefully we can share a beer with our archonic shadows. We do not need to like the way they play the game, but, ultimately, before the sun sets, we need to learn to love them. This might be the most bitter medicine of all; to love the darkness within.

*　*　*

The Gnostic texts of the Nag Hammadi Library are permeated by an asceticism of one degree or another, ranging from the moderate to the severe. *The Gospel of Thomas* declares that those who do not fast from the world will not find the Kingdom of Heaven. Fasting does not simply mean abstaining from food and drink—although, to some extent, this is no doubt required—but rather it refers to a letting go of the fetters of matter, the passions of the mind and the flesh, and everything that binds us to the world of shadows. According to the Gnostic tradition, this includes sexual restraint or abstinence, whether temporarily or permanently. In *The Testimony of Truth* it teaches that the saviour descended from the Pleroma by way of the River Jordan, which immediately turned back on itself, bringing an end to the "dominion of carnal procreation" (p. 617). The *Testimony* makes it clear that reference to the River Jordan is esoteric symbolism for the physical body and the pleasures of the senses. Specifically, the waters of the Jordan refer to the desire for sexual intercourse. The text continues that only someone who completely renounces the things of the world and subdues the passions can realise the truth of God. *The Gospel of Philip* acknowledges the great mystery of marriage, including its carnal expression. Without it, the world could not exist for the world, as humanity experiences it at least, is inherently dependent on people, and people could not exist without marriage (and the procreation that typically results from it).

However, the text cautions that the power of the pure intercourse of the mystical marriage, which occurs in a realm superior to this one, has become defiled in its image on Earth, that is, the carnal marriage. *Philip* makes an unambiguous distinction between what is referred to as the marriage of defilement, fuelled by the carnality of sexual desire, and the undefiled marriage of metaphysical union driven by pure thoughts directed by the will. The marriage of defilement is associated with darkness and the night in which the fire of the passions flickers briefly and then is quickly extinguished. On the other hand, the undefiled marriage is characterised by the day and the holy light, and neither the day nor its light ever sets. Furthermore, only one who accomplishes the rite of the mystical marriage will receive the holy light, and if it is not received in this realm, it cannot be received in any other place. *The Exegesis on the Soul* also makes the same sharp contrast between the mystical union of spirit and soul in the bridal chamber and the marriage of the flesh. The Gnostic teachings on sexuality are, of course, deeply unpopular and, unsurprisingly, commentaries on the Gnostic texts tend to gloss over this aspect of the teachings if, indeed, they make any reference to it at all. There are some who might like to dismiss the teachings of the Nag Hammadi Library, including what they say about sexuality, as merely the "outer" teachings of the Gnostics, and claim that the real, "inner" teachings were reserved for the select, initiated few. The implication is, of course, that the person making such a claim is one of the enlightened few. Yes, secret teachings are often referred to, even in canonical scripture, for example,

> And he said unto them, "Unto you it is given to know the mystery of the kingdom of God, but unto them that are without, all these things are done in parables, that seeing they may see, and not perceive; and hearing they may hear, and not understand; lest at any time they should be converted, and their sins should be forgiven them." (Mark 4:11–12, KJV)

Notwithstanding such claims, or the accusations of the Gnostics' detractors—which must be taken with a liberal dose of salt—if we want to understand the Gnostic tradition, we have little reasonable recourse other than to take the Gnostic texts at face value. The Gnostic schools were extant between the second and fourth centuries CE when the Christian horse race had been run, a winner declared, and the establishment of an institutionalised Church as a means of control was underway. During this time, the Church heresiologists, such as Irenaeus, Hippolytus, Tertullian, Clement, and Origen, set about the condemnation and suppression of the teachings of all other horses in the race, especially those of the Gnostics, who claimed that the divine could be accessed through direct inner experience without the need of a Church as intermediary. Seen in the light of the Church's agenda, the heresiologists' vitriolic attacks against the Gnostics need to be regarded as questionable. (Personally, I am disinclined to take too seriously those who had no qualms about burning others at the stake for simply disagreeing with them over a minor point of theology—although it was never about theology, it was about control.) Whereas claims of a secret inner teaching cannot be disproved, in the face of such claims, a certain amount of caution ought to be observed. Perhaps the true secret teachings are those that are to be found within. Jung claimed that the person who looks outside is a dreamer, and that the person who looks inside for salvation awakens. "When thou prayest, enter into thy closet, and when thou hast shut thy door, pray to thy [God] which is in secret" (Matthew 6:6, KJV). The blatant dismissal of the Gnostics' teachings on sexuality might well be one of those blue pill moments. You can take the blue pill, wake up in your bed, and believe whatever the archons want you to believe.

* * *

Whereas in the Gnostic tradition there is no doubt that the ultimate destination of the Gnostic soul was a return to the Pleroma, the ultimate destination in the *Seven Sermons* is quite different. Indeed, in some respects, Gnostic and Jungian eschatologies take opposing views. Although in his memoirs, *Memories, Dreams, Reflections* (1962)—written very late in his life—Jung speculated about what happens after death, in his public psychological works he avoided statements about the fate of the soul after the death of the physical body. For example, in his "Psychological Commentary on 'The Tibetan Book of the Dead'" (1957), he claimed that we "know desperately little about the possibilities of continued existence of the individual soul after death, so little that we cannot even conceive how anyone could prove anything at all in this respect ... such a proof would be just as impossible as the proof of God (p. 67). However, in his Gnostic vision, the *Seven Sermons*, Jung postulates that the place an individual soul goes to rest after the death of the body is a star located at an inestimable distance in the zenith of the firmament. In the words of musician David Bowie—who some claim was influenced by the Gnostics—there is a star man waiting in the sky. However, rather than him come to meet us, we are to go and meet him. Hopefully, he will not blow our minds. According to Jung, there is one star for each individual and this personal star is both the individual's god and goal. Jung contrasts this world as the dark, chilling moisture of nothingness, ruled by Abraxas, compared to the eternal sunshine of the creative power of the star. Nothing prevents the individual completing the long journey to the distant star at death provided he, or she, can avert his, or her, gaze from what Jung describes as the flaming spectacle of Abraxas (2009). In other words, only succumbing to the pull of the opposites can stop the individual from attaining final repose in the star. For the ancient Gnostics, the task was to seek a return to the original state of the Pleroma prior to the emanation of the first aeons, whereas in Jung's gnosis the task was to aim for the stars, a destination far removed from the original source. Paraphrasing the words of the playwright Oscar Wilde, we are all in the gutter of this archonic world, but some of us are concerned about escaping to, or beyond, the stars.

To some extent Jung's eschatological star god in the *Seven Sermons* feels like an avoidance. He seems to push the problem of the ultimate fate of the individual to somewhere way "out there". In effect, he does not really deal with it adequately. To be fair, the *Seven Sermons* was written in his mid-life when he had only really begun an earnest exploration of his own inner world. He was still in the throes of his confrontation with the unconscious and, no doubt, had not attained the fully individuated state. Perhaps, having not achieved the ultimate goal of psycho-spiritual development and simply not having had the experience—obviously, he had not experienced the after death state—he did not feel qualified to incorporate individual eschatology as a fully worked out, integrated aspect of his Gnostic vision, and included brief, speculative comments only. This ought to be commended for its intellectual honesty, yet the star god finale in the *Seven Sermons* remains somewhat unsatisfactory. Perhaps this explains why the emphasis in the *Seven Sermons* shifts very quickly from a metaphysical focus to a psychological one and, as such, it is not a cosmological process that is being described, but the birth of consciousness. In short, Jung's Gnostic vision, and particularly his psychology, founded in large measure on the former, is at odds with

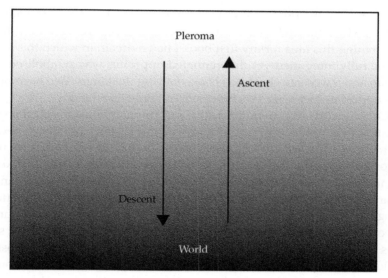

Figure 17. The return to the Pleroma of the Gnostics.

the Gnostics of old in terms of the ultimate goal. For the Gnostics, this world, created in error, was seen as a prison from which humanity was to escape. They thought that we have been cast into this world (descent), without our consent, and remain imprisoned through the archons' deception. We are not here to redeem or transform the world in any way. Our task is simply to extricate ourselves and return to the source (ascent). This is the descent/ascent pattern (Figure 17) of Gnostic soteriology that has been discussed above.

On the other hand, unlike the bidirectional pattern of Gnostic eschatology, in which the path of ascent retraces the steps of the prior path of descent, Jung envisaged a linear psycho-spiritual developmental journey from an unconscious Godhead to a fully realised Self. Jung's Gnostic eschatology of the individual involves a tripartite linear trajectory from 1) the undifferentiated opposites which cancel each other out in the Godhead (Pleroma), through 2) the state of differentiated opposites which give life its spark and allow the world to come into existence, to 3) a final state in which all opposites have been reconciled, integrated, and ultimately unified (the Self). However, the crucial difference between the first and final state is that, rather than the opposites dissolving into one another and cancelling one another out on the return, the final state is one of harmonious balance of the opposites in which they retain at least some degree of differentiation. (When researching this idea for my first book I had a dream in which this idea of the fully integrated-yet-differentiated opposites was symbolised by a man and a woman, cheek-to-cheek, dancing the tango. Two harmonious opposites, perfectly synchronised, but only one dance.)

Consequently, the defining feature of Jungian Gnostic soteriology, one that does not have the same degree of emphasis in the Gnostic texts, is the need for a growth in consciousness in this life. According to the Gnostics we are, metaphorically, nothing more than a bunch of drunken, somnambulist zombies who have fallen prey to the veil of ignorance spun by the archons that keeps us imprisoned in the world of matter. Jung, no stranger to bluntness himself, was somewhat more circumspect in regard to our fallen state, and noted that humanity's worst sin was unconsciousness. Therefore, the key to salvation in Jung's Gnostic vision, which would directly influence his psychology, is to become more conscious. In Gnostic systems, the archons that keep humanity imprisoned are not so much to be seen as evil—although their effects are very much evil—rather they are to be seen as being ignorant, and of a very limited, unfeeling, robotic consciousness. As a result, the key to achieving salvation is not so much overcoming evil, but about becoming more conscious, and this pursuit of increasing consciousness is certainly the direction taken by the soteriological aspects of Jung's gnosis. However, whereas for the Gnostics, gnosis was a means to an end, and that end was escape, for Jung, gnosis, in terms of expanded consciousness, was both the means and the end itself in many ways.

For the Gnostics the return to the Pleroma involved a dissolution of the opposites back to their original, non-differentiated state. However, for Jung, this dissolution posed a great danger and was the sin of unconsciousness, and a retreat back into nothingness and non-existence, in other words, death. As has been noted above, in Jung's view, life is dependent on differentiation. No differentiation, no life, and without life there can be no growth in consciousness. Consciousness demands the differentiation of opposites, and growth in consciousness demands the reconciliation and integration of the opposites. Differentiation of the opposites is what saves humanity from unconsciousness. Yet, in Jung's view all of humanity's problems result from the splitting of opposites in the psyche, both the personal psyche, and the collective psyche. Reconciliation and integration of the differentiated opposites is what

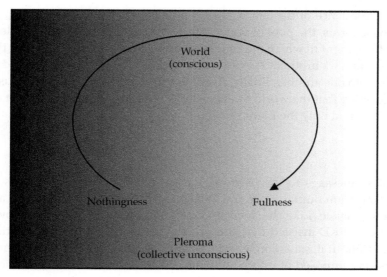

Figure 18. The return in Jung's Gnostic system.

saves humanity from life. If there is to be any concept of a return in Jung's gnosis it would be from the original nothingness of the Pleroma, via the differentiated opposites of creation, returning to the fullness of the Pleroma (Figure 18). Indeed, Jung does refer to the star that each individual goes to after death as their individual pleroma. Alternatively, the goal in Jung's Gnostic system sees the fulfilment of the journey from an unconscious Godhead to the realisation of a fully conscious God.

Given the emphasis on psychological growth in Jung's Gnostic system, the struggle for salvation does not pit aeons against archons as such, but occurs in the unconscious where psychic factors that will save us are opposed by psychic factors that will condemn us. This battle of opposing psychic forces is portrayed symbolically in *The Matrix* in the final showdown between Neo and Agent Smith which begins in the underground (or subway), in other words, the unconscious. In the denouement of their confrontation, Neo charges headlong towards Agent Smith and dives at him; however, there is no collision, rather Neo merges into Agent Smith as if diving into a pool of water. A tumult brews within their entanglement before Agent Smith shatters like a shell, out of which a new Neo is born into light. In Jungian terms, the demiurgic ego dies and the Self is born into the light of consciousness.

The experience of the Self is always a defeat for the ego, said Jung. In Gnostic terms, the pool of water represents the waters that exist below the firmament in which the conflict of human existence occurs. Like the light and dark brothers in *The Gospel of Philip*, Neo and Agent Smith dissolve into one another, finally. Agent Smith shatters like an empty husk, suggesting that the world of the archons is empty, false, nothing but an illusion, and only the Light remains.

* * *

PKD's "message to the listening world" (2008, p. 246) was for us to awaken from our slumber and awaken to gnosis because our lives are in the balance. Like the ancient Gnostics—as well as Jung in his own fashion—PKD insisted that gnosis was the essential factor of salvation and, without it, salvation was not possible. Given his view that the universe is composed of information, he concluded that only information, the gnosis sought by the Gnostics, can save us: "*There is no other road to salvation*" (2001, p. 265, emphasis added). However, a key aspect of gnosis in PKD's view is that the process of attaining gnosis is not the acquisition of something that we never had, but it is, in fact, the act of *anamnesis* (i.e., the loss of forgetfulness), in other words, the remembrance of who we are and where we have come from. He claims that the information that we need is here, covered up, and all we have to do is realise it (2011).

Salvation from what exactly? For PKD, it meant escape from this world, the Black Iron Prison. He claims that God is not responsible for "such a structure of suffering" (ibid., loc. 5775) but, instead, God wishes to liberate us from it and restore us "as part of him" (loc. 5775). A return to the original source is intrinsic to PKD's gnosis. This concept of salvation, along with the notion of a counterfeit phenomenal world, is an inseparable part of his acosmic worldview and features in all of his writings. He adds that the objective he attempts through his written work is the eradication of this world, the achievement of which would go some way to our restoration in the Pleroma.

In a way similar to the Gnostic belief that the individual needed to initiate the process of salvation by preparing the bride to meet the bridegroom, PKD felt that the individual needed to "rebel" (loc. 6806), initially at least, against the Empire in order to instigate salvation. However, once again consistent with the view of the ancient Gnostics,

PKD's view was that gnosis on its own was insufficient for salvation, and that the role of the saviour was essential to restore us to our true state. On our own, we are unable to find the information necessary to escape from the morass of "drugs, communism, and sex and fake plural pathological pseudo worlds" (loc. 8339). Only from the Holy Spirit can we receive gnosis, hence the Christian teaching that we are saved by the grace of God rather than by good works. For PKD, gnosis from above, imparted by the Holy Spirit, resulting in a living plasmate in its cross-bonded, activated form (i.e., the homoplasmate), and accompanied by the sacraments, is the only means of salvation. According to PKD, the saviour draws us up and out of this world. Like the Gnostics before him, but in contrast to Jung, who held a far more world-affirming view, PKD surmised that the world itself cannot be saved, and that we need to be "rescued *off* this dying (toxic, stagnant) world" (loc. 8492). He summarises his metaphysics, and the saviour's role in it, by stating that our minds have been deliberately occluded to blind us to the fact of our imprisonment. This prison is the work of "a power magician-like evil deity" (loc. 8339) who is being opposed by "a mysterious salvific entity which often takes trash forms, and who will restore our lost real memories" (loc. 8339). Yet, despite the dark brutality of PKD's metaphors of the Empire and the Black Iron Prison, and the need to reject them in order to escape, the key to salvation is not to give in to what would be a natural urge to fight the system. In accord with Jung's dictum that what we resist, persists, PKD thought that those who fight against the Empire become "infected by its derangement" (2001, p. 264), resulting in the paradox that, to the extent we defeat the Empire, we become the Empire. Sticking with the viral analogy, he notes that the Empire—the archons—spreads like a virus, imposing its nature on its enemies, and thereby takes control of its human hosts.

This brings to mind a scene from the standout Gnostic myth for modern times, *The Matrix*, in which Agent Smith shares an insight into the human condition. He claims that while trying to classify the human species he realises that they are not actually mammals. Every mammal in this world naturally develops an equilibrium with its habitat and forms part of the ecosystem. Humans, however, do not do this, notes Smith. Instead, humans migrate to an area and continue to multiply until all the earth's resources in that area have been exhausted, forcing humans to relocate to another area and repeat the process. Smith adds, sarcastically, that the other organism that exhibits this behaviour is a virus. Smith concludes that humans are nothing more than a cancer on this planet, a plague that needs to be cured. I know he is the "bad guy", but I cannot help liking Agent Smith, if only just a little bit. I have to give it to him, he has a valid point. We are the virus. We are the Empire and the Black Iron Prison. We are the jailed and our own jailers. We are the archons. However, paraphrasing George Orwell, all humans are archons, but some humans are more archonic than others. How does the body eliminate foreign pathogens? One method is phagocytosis, and although this is not the way the body deals with viruses—let's not let a few medical details get in the way of a good story—it is interesting that PKD uses the analogy of phagocytosis as the means by which the homoplasmate rids the human of its archonic virus.

As noted above, Jung's Gnostic vision involved a teleology at odds with the view of the ancient Gnostics. For the ancients, the created world had no positive purpose for either divinity or humanity. Its only purpose was a malevolent one: as an energy source for the parasitic archons who had created it. For Jung, the purpose of humanity in the world was the creation and expansion of consciousness. Like Jung, PKD's Gnostic vision includes a constructive purpose for the world notwithstanding its counterfeit nature.

In the *Tractates Cryptica Scriptura*, PKD claims that the purpose the One Mind (Godhead) has for the universe is that it serves as a "teaching instrument" (2001, p. 266) for humanity. His acosmic Gnostic perspective leads him to believe that God is not revealed by the world as they have fundamentally different natures. In order to realise God, the world must be abolished. He likens the world to a mask projected by God in order to conceal himself from humanity. Humanity's task, therefore, is to unravel the moral and epistemological puzzles that the world presents in order to "come to life" (2011, loc. 6968). For PKD, the created world is not isomorphic with the Godhead, the two are incompatible, with the world nothing but a "smokescreen" (loc. 6976) which humanity is to eschew rather than make peace with. The task of humanity in the world, therefore, is to learn or, more accurately, relearn how to become isomorphic with the Godhead, in other words, how to return to the original state of the Pleroma.

Like the Gnostics, PKD also couched the return to the Pleroma in terms of a vertical ascent via what he refers to as an orthogonal axis that will be discovered eventually and serendipitously, presumably after much hard work. Yet, once more in accord with the Gnostics, for

PKD the ascent is purely metaphorical for, in reality, the attainment of gnosis means the rediscovery of something we already have. We are already in the Pleroma, we always have been and, rather than a physical ascent, the return involves a movement towards anamnesis and away from amnesia. So, rather than thinking that we have come from the Pleroma and will eventually return to it, it is more correct, according to PKD, to say, "I am part of [the Pleroma] now and always have been" (loc. 4565).

PKD's notion of Gnostic salvation concerns not only the salvation of the individual, it also has a restorative value for the collective. Similar to Jung's view that salvation through the growth of individual consciousness contributes to the collective growth in consciousness in which the Godhead comes to realise itself fully as God, PKD considered the salvation of the individual to have a far greater significance for the system as a whole than it did for the individual (2001). For the individual, gnosis, or anamnesis, results in "a quantum leap in perception, identity, cognition, understanding, world- and self-experience, including immortality" (p. 268). However, each person's restoration contributes to the process of self-repair of the whole entity, the Pleroma.

Another factor in PKD's concept of Gnostic salvation is the redemptive value of chaos as an impetus for change. In his paper, "How to build a universe that doesn't fall apart in two days" (1978), PKD shares a secret that, in his writings, he likes to conceptualise universes that do, indeed, fall apart. He likes the mental stimulation of working through how the characters in his novels will cope with such universes. He confesses to a "secret love" of chaos and mischievously advocates more of it. He claims that order is not always a good thing as it tends to ossify and must, sooner or later, submit to change and the birth of the new. Before the new can be born, the old must perish and die. In the same way that Jung believed that the tension between the opposites was necessary for life, PKD realised that, out of necessity, a certain amount of chaos is required to counterbalance order and to precipitate the change. Chaos is "part of the script of life". He continues that, difficult as it may be, unless we accept this need to change, we die inwardly, growth is stunted, and salvation, if not terminated, is suspended. Order and chaos are opposites which must be reconciled in life. Jung would concur.

CHAPTER TWELVE

Christ and Sophia

When I think of the Supreme Being as inactive neither creating nor preserving nor destroying, I call Him Brahman ... the Impersonal God. When I think of [Her] as active—creating, preserving, destroying, I call [Her] Shakti ... the Personal God. But the distinction between them does not mean a difference. The Personal and the Impersonal are the same thing, like milk and its whiteness, the diamond and its lustre, the snake and its wriggling motion. It is impossible to conceive of the one without the other. The Divine Mother and Brahman are one.

—Ramakrishna, Indian mystic

It is not a coincidence that the words "whole" and "holy" share a common origin. Becoming holy means becoming whole, returning to the One, the Pleroma. If, as both the ancient Gnostics and Jung—and to a lesser extent, PKD—have argued, that salvation demands either a dissolution of all opposites (Gnostic), or their reconciliation and integration (Jung), then, second only to the conscious/unconscious polarity, perhaps there is no pair of opposites in greater need of our urgent attention than the primal syzygy, the male/female dichotomy. It is simply impossible to become whole when one half of that whole, the feminine, is denied. Such has been the extent of the suppression of the feminine—by the institutions of Christianity among others—that it is little wonder that John Lamb Lash, author on the subject of the Gnostic tradition, symbolises the denigration by beginning his work, *Not in His Image* (2006), recounting the brutal murder, by a Christian mob, of the ancient Greek philosopher, Hypatia (born c. 355 CE, died 415)—who became the principal of the Neoplatonic school in Alexandria. Critical to the salvation of humanity is the restoration of the divine feminine, a task which has, with considerable justification, been described as the most important task facing humanity in this century (Ruumet, 2006). Until it is complete, it will remain the most important task of subsequent centuries—assuming humanity has not destroyed itself in the meantime.

A key feature of Gnostic cosmogony is *Barbelo*, the highest female principle. The Great Invisible Spirit thinks, and his first thought, known as forethought, comes into being as Barbelo, his feminine counterpart, the first emanation and foremost of the aeons. In *The Secret Book of John* Barbelo is the reflection of the Spirit who becomes the universal womb out of which everything else proceeds. With her arrival, One becomes Two, and the Mother-Father that subsequently generates all that exists is established. It should be noted that the first thought is the image of the Great Invisible Spirit. In Gnostic thought, it is not humanity that is created in the image of God, it is the first thought, Barbelo, that is the feminine mirror-image of the ultimate divinity. Despite the ineffable nature of the Great Invisible Spirit and Barbelo these non-beings-beyond-being might be tentatively characterised as follows:

Great Invisible Spirit	Barbelo
Male	Female
Father	Mother
Rest	Motion
Emptiness	Fullness
Nothing	Everything
Thinker	First thought
Depth	Silence

The Gospel of Thomas teaches that the divine is motion and rest. Designating rest as male and motion as female is the inverse of the more usual attributions that would see the male principle as active in relation to the more passive, or receptive, female principle. This is not merely contrariness on the part of the Gnostics—although they perhaps had a penchant for that—rather it suggests, not only an inherent enantiodromia—the tendency of a thing to change into its opposite—in the paired opposites, but also points to the indistinct nature of the non-differentiated opposites in the Pleroma where male can be female, and vice versa. PKD also notes this potential for true polar opposites to switch poles. At one point in his *Exegesis*, PKD notes the concept whereby as soon as something exists, it turns into its opposite, which subsequently turns into its opposite, and so on (2011, loc. 10155). Likewise, Jung was no stranger to the concept of enantiodromia. With this in mind, it could be the case that, in order for something to exist it must vibrate, and as the first emanations vibrate at the highest possible frequency, they, consequently, have the capacity to switch polarity frequently and more or less instantaneously. Given that the opposites at the highest level in the Pleroma are differentiated to an infinitesimally small degree, they can hardly be considered distinct at all, hence, the characterisation of Barbelo, the first emanation, as the androgynous "Mother-Father". With the opposites of Thinker and First Thought designated as rest and motion respectively, perhaps we should consider the Great Invisible Spirit to be at rest, a lazy (good-for-)nothing, with feet up, beer in hand, watching the football (Pleroma United vs. Archon Wanderers: I am barracking for the home team), while his partner, the creative power, Barbelo, sets about the serious business of creation.

To assign the male gender (Father)—or the female gender for that matter—to the One, the Great Invisible Spirit, prior to it having thought Barbelo into being, appears to be ontologically incorrect—not to mention sexist. The opposites cannot exist without their counterpart, there is no up without down, no hot without cold, and no male without female. The opposites can only be understood in relation to the other. If everything was hot and nothing was cold, then hot and cold would be meaningless, indeed, even the concept of temperature would be meaningless. If we attempt to define one of the twins of a pair of opposites, we will either refer to a synonym (e.g., "up" will be defined in terms of "higher"), which simply avoids the issue, or we will need to make reference to its opposites (e.g., "up" might be defined in terms of moving from "lower" to "higher"). It follows that the One, on its own, cannot have gender, or any other characteristic for that matter. The One, and any other concept of ultimate divinity, is beyond gender; to assign it gender is meaningless, and fails to understand the fundamental characteristic of the opposites (which seems rather errant on the part of the Gnostics given how crucial the concept of the opposites is to their thesis). The concept of opposites, including gender, only arises when the One becomes Two. Given the ineffability of what is being discussed, gender assignments seem arbitrary and the crucial point, perhaps, is that when the One, the Thinker, thinks Barbelo, the First Thought, into being, there now exists an androgynous pair. This Mother-Father syzygy is the eternal realm—the One is beyond time and beyond being—and the first and highest of the invisible realms of the Pleroma. Only once the One becomes the Two can there exist the dynamic potential between them that leads to creation. Life is born of the spark of opposites according to Jung, and, as the Mother-Father syzygy, Barbelo is the creative power out of which everything else came into being. Out of the interaction of the twin male/female poles within the Mother-Father the process of emanation began. The One, prior to thinking, is the Nothingness of the Pleroma; the Mother-Father is the Fullness of the Pleroma.

Contrary to what appears to be the general view, in Gnostic thought it is Barbelo, rather than Sophia, who is the supreme Divine Feminine. Barbelo is the first aeon, Sophia is the last. Barbelo is the forethought, Sophia is known as afterthought. Whereas Barbelo is Immaculate, Sophia is the rather mischievous child whose error, the desire to create on her own, led to her bastard offspring, the demiurge, and the rest is our history. The demiurge steals some Light from his mother, Sophia, and, when she realises the wickedness of her son's theft, she repents. Her repentance leads to agitation, and this agitation is the vibration on which the created world is founded. If it exists, it vibrates. The demiurge, and his archons, lacked the power to create on their own. They hijacked the creative power of Barbelo, via her daughter Sophia, the demiurge's mother, in order to fashion the created world. The archons' only power comes through their deception. Ashamed at what she had done, Sophia dared not return to the fullness of the Pleroma, but removed herself to the darkest periphery of the Pleroma. Then, when she realises that the archons have created humans in order to farm them for their light, she imparts some of her essence into the humanity. Thus, part of Sophia remains exiled in the lowest realm of the Pleroma, the other part remains trapped in the fallen world. Sophia represents the human soul, split between the worlds of spirit and matter.

* * *

Although the focus of Jung's work was clearly psychological, there was, without doubt, a profound metaphysical undercurrent to it and, over the course of his career, there was a significant shift from the application of psychotherapy for the treatment of neurosis, to the pursuit of psycho-spiritual development, which he termed individuation. This shift mirrored a transition that he observed in his patients as they moved from the first half of life into the second half of life. He claimed that, having treated many hundreds of patients, the fundamental problem for those in the second half of life—which he put at over thirty-five—was the need to find a spiritual orientation to their life, without which they would never be truly healed. Given that his psychology is founded on the Gnostic theme of the opposites, Jung realised that the goal of psycho-spiritual development is not to become "good" or "holy" *per se*, but to become whole. If one accepts the Gnostic view that the path of ascent back to the Pleroma retraces the steps of the path of descent, in other words, the differentiation of opposites needs to be undone, and if one accepts Jung's view that the culmination of psycho-spiritual development requires a reconciliation and integration of all opposites, then wholeness cannot be achieved until the feminine principle, denigrated for so long, is fully restored to its rightful place as co-equal to its male counterpart. Then, and only then, can the necessary integration of the primal male/female syzygy occur.

What does this mean in practice? In the metaphor of the Gnostics, it means preparing the bride to receive the bridegroom. How can the mystical marriage ever be consummated if the bride has been marginalised, forgotten, excluded? *The Gospel of Philip* refers to the union of spirit and soul occurring in the mirrored bridal chamber. This suggests that spirit and soul are mirror images of one another and are to be afforded equal status. Any spiritual practice aimed at the heights in order to receive the spirit must be complemented by work to reclaim the soul. Exactly what the Gnostics did to achieve this union has largely been lost to the past—unless, of course, you know one of the select few initiated into the secret Gnostic teachings. However, with his spiritual heritage firmly rooted in the Gnostic tradition, Jung's process of individuation provides a modern-day method for integrating what has been suppressed, including the disavowed feminine principle. In the language of Jung's psychology, preparing the bride means reconnecting with, and recovering, one's lost soul. For Jung, the spirituality of the feminine principle is earthly and descends; therefore, the reclamation of the soul requires a descent into the chthonic depths of the unconscious. This need for complementary spiritual practice and soul work is symbolised by the tree of which the branches reach up to Heaven, while the roots reach down to the realm of darkness. Only to the extent to which a tree's roots dig down into the earth can its branches reach to the heavens. Without the roots, there can be no branches reaching up to Heaven. The roots come first. In order to ascend, we must first descend. The image of the tree also points to an overcoming of duality and a return to the Pleroma: it is the same tree above and below the ground. Authentic spirituality must be founded on a psychology that recognises the soul and works to liberate the living soul from the imprisonment in the world of the animal soul. This is not to suggest that the psychology must be complete before spirituality can begin, only that psychological development, and soul work, must be one step ahead of spiritual practice. The bridegroom will only appear to the extent that the bride has been prepared. Spirit can only be received to the extent that the animal soul has become a living soul. Without the necessary work to retrieve the soul, any form of psycho-spiritual development is merely a form of what is referred to as spiritual bypassing.

Spiritual bypassing is a term introduced in the early 1980s by Buddhist teacher and psychotherapist, John Welwood, to refer to the phenomenon of using spiritual practice as a way of denying and avoiding one's humanity. He coined the term in response to what he saw as the widespread "occupational hazard" of people within spiritual communities using their spiritual practice to "avoid facing unresolved emotional issues, psychological wounds, and unfinished developmental tasks" (Fosella & Welwood, 2011). (Personally, I have always found the term to be a misnomer; it is not spirit that is being bypassed, it is psyche, or soul, with all its rawness and messiness that the person is trying to bypass.)

Welwood describes spiritual bypassing as a premature—and therefore, doomed—attempt to transcend to spiritual realms without first having dealt with the "raw and messy side of our humanness" (ibid.). At a psychological level, spiritual bypassing acts as a defence mechanism, seeking to circumvent all those things that we would rather not deal with—psychological challenges, relationship issues, etc.—because they are too emotionally painful, socially unacceptable, or do not fit with the image we have about ourselves or like to project out to the world, and so on. At a deeper level, from a Gnostic perspective, spiritual bypassing results in a failure to address all the things that keep us clinging to the animal soul and further disconnected from the living soul we inherited from the Pleroma.

Psycho-spiritual therapist and author, Robert Augustus Masters, believes the pervasiveness of the problem among those actively pursuing a spiritual life is partly due to both our collective and individual aversion to admitting to, addressing, and resolving our pain. Given what he sees as the normalisation of pain-avoidance within our culture, spiritual bypassing insidiously takes hold without being noticed. Masters (2016) catalogues a number of different ways in which he has observed spiritual bypassing manifesting—including, for example, pronounced detachment, emotional repression, overemphasis on the positive, being overcritical of one's shadow, valuing spiritual concerns at the expense of personal issues, and overestimating one's spiritual development.

Welwood notes that one of the most pernicious consequences of spiritual bypassing is that is leads to a dangerous and debilitating schism between a person's spiritual life and his, or her, everyday humanity, in which the former is valued to the detriment of the latter. This sets up an imbalance in a range of pairs of opposites: the connection to an impersonal concept of divinity is honoured over personal human relatedness, transcendence is pursued and embodiment disparaged, the virtue of non-attachment is used to deny and avoid legitimate emotional needs, and so on (Fosella & Welwood, 2011). As was noted in the discussion on Jung's concept of the opposites above, the consequence of favouring one pole of a pair of opposites is that the disavowed pole of the pair of opposites is repressed, and anything repressed falls into the unconscious where its effects can show up in unforeseen, unwanted, and dangerous ways. Spiritual practice can only be truly effective if it proceeds in parallel with due regard to our fundamental human needs. However, any gains in spiritual practice are not lost. As Thoreau said, if we have built castles in the air, our work need not be lost. The air is where our spiritual castles should be, we simply have to remember to put the necessary psychological foundations underneath them. In the words of the saviour:

> Therefore everyone who hears these words of mine and puts them into practice is like a wise man who built his house on the rock.

> The rain came down, the streams rose, and the winds blew and
> beat against that house; yet it did not fall, because it had its foun-
> dation on the rock. But everyone who hears these words of mine
> and does not put them into practice is like a foolish man who built
> his house on sand. The rain came down, the streams rose, and the
> winds blew and beat against that house, and it fell with a great
> crash. (Matthew 7:24–27, KJV)

Spiritual bypassers are like the man who built his house on the sand.
The rains and winds that batter us in the course of everyday life will
wash and blow away the tottering edifices of their spiritual practice.

Masters (2016) is of the view that an authentic spirituality does
not occur in a "bubble of immunity" from life's problems, but is an
arduous task involving a "vast fire of liberation" which takes place
in a crucible of both heat and light. He adds that whereas we like
the light, we are averse to the heat, and he quotes Holocaust survivor
and psychiatrist, Viktor Frankl, who said that, "What gives light must
endure burning." Similarly, Jung taught that we must pass through
the inferno of the passions in order to overcome them. In contrast to
the Gnostics, whose goal was to escape from this prison world and
return to the Pleroma, Jung believed that life needed to be lived to
the full. Only by living life can we be freed from it (2009). However,
there is no growth in consciousness without pain, and unfortunately,
most people will do anything in order to avoid facing their own soul,
according to Jung. Likewise, in *The Gospel of Thomas*, the saviour says
that whoever is near to him is near to the fire. To realise the reunion
of spirit and soul necessitates that one endures the fire. It is incumbent upon every true Gnostic to burn away all that gets in the way of
liberating the living soul. In a not dissimilar vein, Western Buddhist
nun, teacher, and author, Pema Chödrön (2000), teaches that we can
only find the indestructible part of ourselves to the extent that we
repeatedly expose ourselves to the annihilation of our false sense of
self. In Gnostic terms, the indestructible within is the divine spark
and its counterpart is the living soul. Paraphrasing Chödrön, only to
the extent that we descend into the unconscious and expose ourselves
over and over to the annihilation of the animal soul can we recover
the lost living soul.

* * *

A Danish man is going to clean out a rat-infested oven. He is a former builder, a long-time meditator, and lives in an eco-community that practises permaculture and sustainable living. No one in the community offers to help so I do. The oven is full of rat shit. As we start cleaning the oven, I cut my finger and blood flows. As I return to cleaning, two rats, one after the other, run out of the oven. Then a tree snake slithers across the path between us. We both step back from the snake and it retreats. Then it comes back out and crosses the path between us.

(Author's dreamworld, January 2017)

Despite having practised the spiritual discipline of meditation for many years, the man does not seek the flight of the mystic alone. He is grounded in the world, and is prepared to deal with the raw and messy side (cleaning a rat-infested oven) of our humanness. He is not a spiritual bypasser. Two men, two rats, two snakes; duality, duality, duality. I associate the fact that the man is Danish with physicist Niels Bohr (mentioned above) who included the Taoist yin/yang symbol in his coat of arms, thus further reinforcing the theme of duality. This world is predicated on the opposites, in other words, duality.

The snake appears twice, and given that it is a *tree* snake, clearly symbolises the caduceus, twin serpents entwined around a wooden staff (Figure 19). Churton (2015) suggests that the serpent is a symbol of Sophia, and that something similar to the Eastern discipline of kundalini yoga may have been central to the Gnostics'—specifically the Sethians'—spiritual practice. In an instance of the microcosm mirroring the macrocosm, the Gnostic creation and redemption myth is, from the individual Gnostic's perspective, to be seen as an event taking place not in the cosmos, but within the awakened being of the Gnostic. In this view, the Light of the Pleroma, in seed form, enters through the crown of the head and descends to the lower regions, specifically the genitals, which are governed by the ignorance of the archons who enslave humanity to the cycle of birth and death. When the Light-seed enters the head in its original state it is pure, but it turns into "poison" when it descends to the genitals. Salvation involves Sophia, as serpent, redeeming the seed from above, and redirecting it back up the spinal column (tree) through the chakras to the pineal gland in the head, the gateway to the Pleroma. "As Moses lifted up the serpent in the wilderness; even so must the Son of man be lifted up" (John 3:14, KJV). Seen in this light, the descent of the Light-seed down through the crown of the head is, in Gnostic terms,

Figure 19. The caduceus.

the descent of the emissary from the realm of Light, and the restoration of Sophia is the redirection of the Light-seed, which descends as water, from the lower regions, the genitals, up the spinal column, as fire, to the pineal gland, and back to its source in the Pleroma. This is the Gnostic resurrection. On Earth, Jesus's relationship with the "redeemed whore" Mary Magdalene mirrors the union of Christ and the redeemed Sophia in the Pleroma (Churton, 2015, loc. 3149). Jesus is said to have cast seven devils out of Mary Magdalene (Mark 16:9), and this is may well be a reference to a clearing of the seven chakras situated along the spine in Eastern systems. The awakened Gnostic, either male or female, who has raised the serpent, can realise the reunion of Christ and Sophia.

Quoting the medieval *Kularnava Tantra*, Churton notes that, from the male's perspective, "If liberation could be attained simply by having intercourse with a [female partner], all living beings in the world would be liberated by having intercourse with women" (loc. 2487), before adding that both knowledge and technique of what is required are crucial. His view seems to be that liberation can be achieved through actual sexual intercourse, provided that the partners maintain the correct state of mind. The Gnostic texts of the Nag Hammadi Library appear to suggest otherwise.

* * *

Although the terminology was different, Jung was well aware of the imperative to avoid spiritual bypassing. Recognising that everything that is differentiated out of the Pleroma is a pair of opposites, he realised that God and the devil form a pair of opposites. There cannot be one without the other. In *The Red Book*, he accepts that if he wants God, then he must have the devil also. One cannot attain the light above without first addressing the demons in the darkness of the depths, that is, by bringing the darkness into the light of consciousness. Preparing the bride, recovering the soul, requires working with the darkness of the unconscious.

The contents of the unconscious, due to the very fact that they are unconscious—therefore unknown and, to some extent, ultimately unknowable—are indistinct and tend to become contaminated with one another. Thus, the denied and forsaken soul, accessible only through the unconscious, tends to become intermingled with other unconscious factors. Consequently, the living soul can only be reclaimed by delving into the shadowy depths of the unconscious, and this rescue mission means addressing our demons and wrestling with the darkness that holds her captive. In the words of Jung, it involves kindling the light of consciousness in the darkness of our being and bringing the darkness into the light. "Have no fellowship with the unfruitful works of darkness, but rather reprove them" (Ephesians 5:11, KJV). Although the process of Jungian psycho-spiritual development is anything but linear, the first step invariably involves working with what Jung called the shadow.

In Jungian psychology, the shadow is the term used for the unconscious composite of all the disowned parts of the personality. It consists of all aspects of who we are and would rather not deal with, and therefore, get swept under the psychological carpet. As its name suggests, the shadow is the dark side of the personality and is precisely the aggregation of all the parts of our individuality that spiritual bypassers seek to avoid. As a unit, these rejected aspects of our psychological make-up can function as an autonomous complex. Jung argued that anything real casts a shadow that is just as real as the thing itself. To the extent that there is any reality to our general sense of self—the ego personality with its accompanying persona, the mask of the ego personality that we display to the world— then there is a shadow complex that is every bit as real.

In his view of the psyche as a self-regulating organism, Jung considered the shadow to compensate for any one-sidedness in the ego/

persona structure and this can have both positive and negative aspects. However, due to its repressed and unconscious nature, the shadow typically operates in a way that would be considered negative.

Foreshadowing Jung's later work, one of the best explorations of the human shadow in literature is Robert Louis Stevenson's novel, *The Strange Case of Dr. Jekyll and Mr. Hyde*. Stevenson presents a perfect depiction of the vague (i.e., largely unconscious) nature of the shadow:

> He is not easy to describe. There is something wrong with his appearance; something displeasing, something downright detestable. I never saw a man I so disliked, and yet I scarce know why. He must be deformed somewhere; he gives a strong feeling of deformity, although I couldn't specify the point. (1886)

Stevenson notes that although the human is, perhaps, a "mere polity of multifarious, incongruous and independent denizens", these various factors largely coalesce into two opposing natures. In what he describes as a primitive duality, humans are not one, but two. We are commingled out of both good and evil, simultaneously both, the realisation of which he likens to a dreadful shipwreck. Such can be the power of an encounter with the shadow.

Jung identified two dimensions to the shadow: one personal, and the other, archetypal. The personal shadow consists of the disavowed parts of the individual's personality, whereas the archetypal shadow is the rejected aspects of the human collective. The personal shadow is our own private demiurge, and the archetypal shadow is the Gnostic demiurge and his archons. Recovering the living soul demands that we address not only our personal shadow, but also the darkness of the collective demiurgic shadow to the extent that it touches us. As noted above, *The Gospel of Philip* teaches that as long as the root of evil remains hidden, its power over us will persist. It is powerful because we do not recognise it. When it is recognised, in other words, when it is brought into the light of consciousness, it dies. *Philip* exhorts us to dig down to get at the root of evil and pull it out of our hearts by the root. Its uprooting is in its recognition. As long as it is ignored, it takes root in our heart and dominates us. We become its slaves, and such is our enslavement that we are compelled to do things that we do not want to do, and are unable to do the things we want to do. If we are not conscious of the archons within us, they fall into the shadow, and that suits the archons just fine. From there they can carry on their diabolical activities unhindered. Liberating the soul begins with recognising the darkness.

* * *

While working on this chapter, I had the following dream:

> I go with a group of people to prepare for what I think is a long-distance running race. I'm told that my experience on the Camino in Spain last year was good preparation for this even though this feels more like a twenty-four-hour running race rather than a multi-day, long-distance hike. I go to my locker to get my running gear but when I open the locker door there is just another door. I open it and there is another door. This repeats a few times and I can't get into the locker. I look in a couple of adjacent lockers and they are the same. The locker door opens to reveal only another door. I'm frustrated that I won't be able to use my running gear for the race. A woman shows up to help out with some alternative gear. Notably, I'll be competing in jeans rather than shorts, and my shoes aren't really running shoes.
>
> However, it seems to be a long-distance adventure race rather than a running race. Ultimately, the "race", which is not really a race, is the same for everyone but each participant has his own set of checkpoints to get to over the course of the race. We are given clues to the next checkpoint only and we have to find our way there, where we receive something, including clues to the next checkpoint.
>
> As we head off, I think of having just returned from an amazing adventure trip to Alaska. I'm telling some colleagues about what a wonderful time I had. A friend and I are thinking of buying a log cabin in Alaska and running adventure holidays including fishing trips.
>
> My first checkpoint is a park in the city which seems to be Glasgow. There is a small tourist information kiosk where a few participants are lined up to get some information on how to get to their checkpoint. Impatiently, I want to press on, but think I should stop and ask for directions. The woman at the kiosk tells me the park is just across the street and around the corner. I have to cross Donaldson St. to get there. I thank the woman in Spanish. Why? Do I think I'm in Spain or South America? This is Glasgow, the woman speaks my language.
>
> I enter the park and look around for my clue. The park seems to be partitioned off into walled-off gardens. I have to climb up on the walls to

see into the next garden. This could make things harder. I look around and find some items that have been left there for me. One item is a symbol of a knight on a quest for the Holy Grail, or a pilgrim. I want to take this with me. It promises that sainthood will be conferred on me when I complete the journey. Another item is an outstanding bill for a small amount (for hospitality received at the place where the journey started perhaps).

Darkness is falling rapidly and I wonder if we will spend the night somewhere or continue the journey through the night. I see a note that states that my guide will show up about 8:15 pm to take me to a hotel. Soon a young woman appears. Her name is Irya. She has fair, or blonde, hair and is wearing glasses. She vaguely reminds me of the young Romanian woman I met briefly on the Camino last year, except Irya's hair is light rather than dark. Irya is lively, enthusiastic, helpful, encouraging; everything one would want in an adventure tour guide.

(Author's dream journal, December 2016)

I requested a dream that would highlight some of the themes of this chapter. This dream is the result. However, much of its content is personal in nature and not relevant to this discussion. Nevertheless, the extraneous details—as far as this work is concerned—have been included in the dream narrative to illustrate the pertinent details within the context of the dream while retaining the integrity of the dream.

This dream came while I was not only working on this chapter, but also reading PKD's *The Divine Invasion*, in which the leading female character, who represents Sophia, is called Zina, a Romanian name. Given the reference to a Romanian woman in the dream, I assumed Irya, which I had never heard before, was an Eastern European woman's name. However, Irya is a Sanskrit male name meaning powerful or energetic. In the dream, Irya is female, rather than male, and this suggests that her name is pointing to its meaning rather than its gender. Thus, Irya represents the creative power of the feminine principle. I could identify Irya as an anima figure, but that would be arid intellectualisation; Irya is the soul, my soul, and the daughter of Sophia. The dream suggests that sainthood will be conferred on anyone who rediscovers and follows their soul, through the labyrinth (Figure 20) of twists and turns and checkpoints, to the journey's end.

My chess dream (see above) and this dream present the journey of life as a game and an adventure race, respectively, both compensating

Figure 20. The labyrinth symbolising the odyssey of life.

for the dark pessimism that can, all too easily, be read into the Gnostic message. The Gnostic tradition has taken hold of me, and I accept it with considerable reluctance; its message speaks of a darkness I wish was not so.

* * *

PKD was also aware of the imperative need to integrate the feminine principle. In his *Exegesis*, he recounts a dream in which he claims the dual nature of Christ is revealed to him. In the dream, PKD is presented with an image that he describes as a medieval diptych (i.e., an altarpiece that consists of two hinged wooden panels), of which the right hand panel illustrates the inner nature of Christ. PKD likens this symbol to Michelangelo's painting of the Delphic sibyl and notes that it is anno-tated with the words "SHE" and "SECRET".

PKD concludes from this dream that the female aspect of Christ, which he regards as the superior part, is Holy Wisdom (i.e., Sophia). He continues by expressing his eager anticipation for what he sees as the next cycle of human evolution which will include a composite of the masculine and feminine principles as depicted in his dream. He claims that the feminine side will dominate and that is all right with him (2011). PKD's reimaged Christ is, in fact, a male/female, Christ/Sophia, syzygy, physically male on the outside and spiritually female on the inside, combining what he sees as the best of both, "masculine posture of assertiveness plus feminine love and warmth" (loc. 4287). This is perhaps a man's description of a male/female spiritual syzygy experienced through an encounter with his anima. A woman's experience of the same male/female syzygy might be quite different. For PKD, this is the incarnation of Sophia, "two persons, or rather ... two essences! Forming one person!" (loc. 4303). Sophia is Christ; they are one and the same (2001, p. 175). PKD then goes on to assert his conception of the Christ/Sophia syzygy as Gnostic, claiming that it is only Gnosticism that "denies the patriarchal Jewish-Christian religion and enshrines Sophia as the creator goddess" (2011, loc. 4370). He continues that his "experience of the lady—it is exactly Gnostic. *None else*" (loc. 4370, emphasis in original), before adding that his revelations indicate that everything leads back to her, and that this is the essence of Gnosticism. Except that he is not quite right. Whereas he is correct to afford Christ and Sophia equal status in order that the primal syzygy is correctly symbolised in male/female balance, he is incorrect in Sophia's role as creator. Sophia, as the daughter of the creative power of Barbelo, is a creator goddess, but this world is the flawed handiwork of the demiurge and the archons who have appropriated some of Sophia's power.

Another important component in the restoration of Sophia in PKD's vision is that his work was a lifelong search for his lost soul which he projected onto his twin sister who died shortly after birth, and whose loss must have had a profound effect on him. He states that his search in this world, and in all other worlds as well, is for his sister, who he describes as his female counterpart. He believed that she lived on after her physical death and that, one day, he would be reunited with her (loc. 8395).

* * *

In today's world, any reverence for the feminine principle is invariably linked to environmental concerns and associated with worship of Mother Earth or the Divine Feminine. It should be noted that the Gnostics did not equate Sophia, or any other feminine aeon, with Mother Earth. Indeed, there is no concept of Mother Earth for the Gnostics; rather, this world is a flawed world fashioned by the demiurge and the archons. Any attempts to appropriate the Gnostics' veneration of Sophia, and co-opt it into some kind of syncretic New Age Gaia worship is an egregious misinterpretation of the Gnostics' position. Worship of Mother Earth did not form any part of the ancient Gnostics' reverence for the divine feminine. Note, it is not being argued that the Gnostics were "right" and the New Agers "wrong"—a true Gnostic would attempt to include and transcend such black-and-white propositions—it is simply being pointed out that conflating the Gnostic Sophia with the *physical* earth, or any metaphysical substrate of the earth, is glaringly inaccurate, not to mention disgraceful culturo-religious misappropriation. Nevertheless, the view that this world is a dream world, and a prison, and a corrupt world created in error should not be seen as granting the Gnostic free licence to have a flagrant disregard for environmental concerns. On the contrary, the dream is real for as long as it lasts, and this environment nourishes our physical bodies while we are here. *The Gospel of Philip* states that the resurrection can only be attained in this world, so it follows that the physical body is the instrument for its attainment. It is a duty to protect the environment that sustains us.

CHAPTER THIRTEEN

The imagination and the third eye

Imagination is the only weapon in the war against reality.
—Lewis Carroll, *Alice in Wonderland*

It should be clear by now that the main thesis of this book is that, in the Gnostic tradition, a return to the Pleroma is founded on the reintegration and dissolution of the opposites which were differentiated when the fullness of the Pleroma emanated out of its depths, and were later rent asunder by the demiurge and the archons when they created the world of matter. The previous chapter explored the reconciliation of the primal male/female syzygy, spirit and soul, or bride and groom. However, there is an even more fundamental pair of opposites that need to be dissolved in order for the Pleroma to be realised. The return to the Pleroma includes the dissolution of *all* opposites and, paradoxically, this also includes the Pleroma/not Pleroma dichotomy, a split which is often expressed in the separation that is inherent in, or at least implied by, the spatial metaphors of above and below, higher and lower, within and without, and so on. In Jung's Gnostic vision, the Pleroma is simultaneously transcendent and immanent, up there and in here, far removed from creation, yet pervading all of creation.

In *The Gospel of Mary*—generally considered to be Gnostic, although not appearing in the Nag Hammadi Library—Mary asks the saviour whether a vision is seen through the soul or through the spirit, to which the saviour responds that it is the mind that sees the vision. It is the mind that grants a person access to higher spiritual realms, and the faculty of mind required for this purpose is the imagination. The deeply spiritual Scottish naturalist, John Muir (1838–1914)—who experienced God through the natural world and who was instrumental in the establishment of the first national park in the US—thought that the power of the imagination could make us infinite. Similarly, Einstein said that logic could take us from A to B, but the imagination could take us everywhere. He felt that, in contrast to the intellect and the knowledge it can attain, which is limited to all we currently know and understand, the imagination is unlimited, and can embrace the entire world and beyond, including everything that could possibly be known and understood—and everything that we could never understand with a limited human intellect as well, no doubt. It ought to be stressed that it is the imagination functioning in its intuitive capacity that is being discussed here. Paraphrasing Einstein once more, the intuitive mind should be recognised as a sacred gift, whereas the rational mind should be relegated to the role of faithful servant. Unfortunately, we have become victims to the entrenched attitude that honours the servant while neglecting the gift of the intuitive imagination. The imagination is the vehicle that can take us anywhere, including into the spiritual realms "out" there, or "up" there. It can also take us "in" here, or "down" there, into the depths of the soul. The imagination is the instrument through which the above and below, the inner and outer, and the Pleroma and the created world can be reconciled and integrated. The imagination is the means of our salvation. It is the only weapon in the war against the false reality imposed by the archons.

The saviour in *Mary* teaches that the human mind that receives visions exists between spirit and soul. Similarly, in the *Seven Sermons*, Jung describes the human as the gateway through which gods, daimons, and souls can pass from the endless space of the outer world to the innermost infinity of the inner world. The outer world of gods and daimons is the spiritual dimension of its psychological counterpart, the collective unconscious. Fundamentally, the world of gods and daimons is identical with the collective unconscious. If there is any difference, it is one of vibrational frequency only, their essences are the same.

PKD also saw humanity poised between two realms connected by the human mind. In one of his visions recounted in his *Exegesis*, he describes two realms, our world, which he terms "sublunar", and the heavenly realm, which he refers to as "supralunar". These realms can be bridged by way of "a polyencephalic means" (2011, loc. 6024)—in other words, a many-brained mind—which he characterises as heterogeneous. He claims that at either end of the bridge there are saints who facilitate the connection; in our sublunar world there are saints in human form, and at the supralunar end there are saints who have died and passed over into Heaven. God, as the Holy Spirit, is the medium that connects the two realms. Given his holographic view in which the Black Iron Prison and the Palm Tree Garden function as the two laser sources which together generate our illusory world as the holographic universe between the two, it follows that humanity is located in the liminal space between the PTG and the BIP where the work of integration, and, ultimately, dissolution, of them can be done. In both Jung's and PKD's Gnostic view, humanity, through its faculty of the imagination, is the portal that connects the above with the below, the outer with the inner, as well as the spirit with the soul. This concept of the opposites being reconciled in the human imagination situated between the opposites is symbolised in my chess dream recounted above in which the exchange of prisoners, that is, the dialectic interchange that leads to the reconciliation of the warring sides, occurs in the neutral territory between them. *The Gospel of Philip* states that the resurrection can only be attained in this life, it cannot be attained in death. Only in the imagination of the human mind, poised between the opposites, can the integration and dissolution of the opposites be accomplished.

As for the concept that our world is nothing but a dream world lacking any substantial reality, then the faculty of that dream is either the collective, or some kind of transpersonal, imagination. If, as PKD asserts, it is the collective imagination and we are co-creators of this illusory dream world, then why are we dreaming the BIP into existence? Kastrup (2011) answers this question by suggesting that if our consensual reality is imagined into existence, then it would, out of necessity, have to be the "compound result of multiple imaginations at work simultaneously ... [in which] no individual imagination could independently determine the resulting outcome" (loc. 1507). Our experienced reality would be the collective thought patterns projected onto a "multidimensional fabric of space-time". In this model, consensual reality is seen as a "complex amalgamation of [our] collective dreams" (loc. 27) which, as an amalgamation, might bear little resemblance to any given individual's projection. He then explains why we continue to dream the same dream by suggesting that, given that our reality is not what we are projecting as an individual, we assume that reality is an "objective, standalone phenomenon" (loc. 27) outside our control, which, coupled with our "instinctive and visceral need for closure" (loc. 27), leads to a longing for reassurance that we are more than mere "puppets of a dispassionate cosmic process" (loc. 27). This results in an innate expectation of consistency in our experience of reality which, in turn, causes us to imagine previously encountered patterns of perception. Consequently, our imaginations tend to reinforce our learned expectations and, because we perceive the same patterns, we collectively co-create the consistency we long for. In time, consensual reality behaves in accordance with our shared expectations, and we "invent the concepts of cause and effect to model the empirically observable correlations present in the manifested pattern of dreamed up reality" (loc. 69). In short, we all end up dreaming the same dream over and over. Consequently, we end up feeling like "puppets in a cosmic play" (loc. 108) for which we had no input in the writing of the script. As the shared dream is now so entrenched its momentum has become unassailable, so that "no outcast, however determined" (loc. 115) can succeed in projecting a different reality independently. If this model is correct then, in response to the New Age bumper-sticker aphorism that claims that "You create your own reality", one would have to respond that "*You* do not create your own reality, *we*, collectively, create your reality". As a member of "we", you, of course, get to participate in the creating, but whereas you might be the predominant influence in your own sphere, your influence, like everyone else's, is minimal in the wider scheme of things. On the other hand, collectively, we *do* create our reality. However, as PKD points out, we are the archons—as well as being the archons' slaves—and it is our minds, under the influence of our archonic selves, that are continuously dreaming this prison world into existence. If this is so, then we need to dream a better dream, and quickly. In the final scene of *The Matrix*, Neo suggests that this world can remain our cage or it can become our chrysalis. In order to be free, we cannot change the cage, we have to change ourselves. However, once we change ourselves, the cage will no longer exist in the dream.

A striking parallel of the Gnostic idea of humanity as a bridge between spirit and soul can be found in the related, but diverse, group of spiritual traditions generally referred to as shamanism. Common to many shamanic traditions is a tripartite cosmology in which the cosmos is divided into three worlds: the upper world (Heaven), the lower world (underworld), and the middle world (our world). The three worlds are all important, and the terms "upper" and "lower" are spatial *metaphors*, and not to be considered as value judgements of their relative significance. Each world is an intrinsic part of the shamanic whole. Together, the three worlds form a shamanic trinity. Like a stool which requires three legs in order to stand, shamanic cosmology stands on these three worlds.

The upper world, which is also regarded as the heavens or the celestial domain, is the spiritual realm. It is the home of spirit guides and ancestors. In terms of consciousness, it is the realm of what might be considered superconsciousness. In Gnostic terms, the upper world is the fullness of the Pleroma, with the aeons the correlates of the shamanic spirit guides. The lower world, or underworld, is the realm of animal, vegetable, and mineral spirits. It is the home of what is referred to in the shamanic traditions as power animals, or animal guides, as well as the spirits of the trees, rivers, and mountains. It ought to be noted that the shamanic lower world should not be equated with the Western concept of hell. There is no direct parallel of the lower world in Gnostic cosmology. Fundamentally, there are only two realms in Gnostic cosmology, the Pleroma, and the created world. However, in Jung's Gnostic system, in terms of consciousness, the lower world is the unconscious. The lower world, along with the upper world, belongs to a reality that is distinct from the normal, consensual reality of our everyday world. Unlike the everyday world, which is experienced through the normal, waking state, the lower and upper worlds are accessed, typically, through altered states of consciousness, for example, dreams, visions, meditation, trance, and so on. The middle world is, in effect, our everyday world of ordinary, so-called reality. However, it is perhaps best not to think of it as being identical with our physical world (as we perceive it), but rather to consider the middle world to be the vibrational frequency in which the physical world manifests. The middle world is phenomenologically the world of ordinary, waking state consciousness. In Gnostic terms it is the created world of the archons. It is the world in which Neo, in the guise of Thomas A. Anderson, software developer with a social security number, pays his taxes and helps his landlady take out her garbage. It is the world where publicans, sinners, tax collectors, and assorted riff-raff abound. It is the place where the Empire imposes its Black Iron Prison and where we render unto Caesar.

In shamanic traditions, as well as numerous world mythologies, the three worlds are often symbolised by a tree known as the World Tree. The World Tree connects the three worlds: the lower world, symbolised by the tree roots, are connected to the upper world, symbolised by the tree's branches, by the middle world, symbolised by the tree's trunk. Closely associated with the World Tree is the concept of the *Axis Mundi* (the world axis), the central axis that connects the lower world to the upper world via the middle world, symbolically represented by the tree's trunk connecting the roots to the heavens. The axis mundi is considered to be the centre of the world and like the centre of the Empedocolean circle, the axis mundi is considered to be everywhere. As such, any tree can represent the World Tree; to the druid his oak tree, to the Native American her birch tree, and so on. Through altered states of consciousness, the shaman uses the axis mundi as the gateway with which to access the upper and lower worlds and return to the middle world with specific information and healing retrieved from those realms. The tree metaphor used above in describing the need for soul work is none other than the World Tree of shamanic traditions.

It has already been noted above that the Gnostic figure of Abraxas symbolises the possibility of uniting the upper world, the Pleroma, with the created world, and the World Tree of shamanism does a very similar task with virtually identical symbolism. For example, in the Incan tradition, which might be considered to be a form of shamanism, the upper, middle, and lower worlds are represented by the condor, the jaguar, and the serpent respectively. Like Abraxas, who unites the spiritual realm, symbolised by a bird, with the lower world, symbolised by a serpent, via the middle realm of our world, represented by a human torso, similarly the Incans saw their three worlds represented by a bird, mammal, and serpent. The upper world of the condor (bird) and the lower world of the serpent are united in the middle world of the jaguar. Likewise, Jung believed that the world of the bird and the world of the serpent only meet within humanity. It was the tension of the opposites between the upper and lower worlds which brought creation into existence. He said that anyone who wanted to become had to undergo what he described as the battle between the bird and the serpent (2009). In other words, human existence occurs in the middle world where the opposites of bird and serpent are pitted against one another. However, unlike the shamanic tripartite model, Gnostic cosmology is dual and rather than the middle world and its human inhabitants bridging the upper and lower worlds, humanity is seen as the interface, or portal, that bridges two worlds.

The Gospel of Philip teaches that truth cannot be perceived directly from within this world, but only indirectly by means of symbols and images. Those in the world (i.e., humanity) cannot receive the truth in any other way. Similarly, the products of the imagination are, in essence, visual, the underlying nature of which is archetypal (Jung, 1957a). The images from the unconscious, mediated by the imagination, are the means by which the truth is perceived. Philip then makes a distinction between rebirth and an image of rebirth adding that the former can only be achieved by means of the latter. It is the *image* of rebirth that is the way to be reborn in the Pleroma. This is the resurrection: mirroring the harmonious, perfectly balanced union of the primal syzygy in the Pleroma through the rite of the mystical marriage in the bridal chamber within by means of the imagination. Philip continues that one who has received the power of the cross, alternatively, the power of the right and the left, in other words, one who has reunited spirit and soul, symbolically, is no longer a Christian but a Christ. The saviour comes to make the lower like the upper, and the outer like the inner. Likewise, The Gospel of Thomas teaches that the Pleroma will only be realised when the inner and the outer, and the upper and the lower, and the male and the female, have been integrated so that no distinction exists between them. The place where they meet and the integration takes place is in the human. The cross is not a symbol of Christ's torture and death; it is a symbol of the reunion of spirit and soul, upper and lower, outer and inner—and, by extension, all opposites—the mirror-image of the divine harmony of the non-differentiated syzygies in the Pleroma. This reunion of spirit and soul, through the imagination, occurs only in the human who has realised Christ. Only when the bride has been prepared by elevating the soul from an animal soul to a living soul, and the bridegroom, the emissary from the Pleroma with its salvific gnosis, has been received, can the mystical marriage be consummated by the power of the imagination. For the Gnostic, this is Christ-realisation, the way, the truth, and the life, without which no one returns to the Pleroma.

As noted above, the escape from this world and the return to the Pleroma requires an ascent through a series of planes patrolled by the archons who try to intercept the Gnostic and keep him, or her, imprisoned in the fallen world. *The Gospel of Philip* teaches that the archons cannot see a person who wears the perfect light, and therefore cannot prevent that person's ascension. This body of light is created in the mystery of union. Only once spirit and soul are reunited in the bridal chamber does the Gnostic don the garment of perfect light that protects him, or her, from the archons during the ascent back to the Pleroma. According to PKD (2001), the bridal chamber, where the mystical marriage takes place, is located in the pineal gland. In various schools of mysticism, the pineal gland is often associated with what is referred to as the "third eye". "The light of the body is the eye: if therefore thine eye be single, thy whole body shall be full of light" (Matthew 6:22, KJV). When the mystical union occurs in the third eye, then the divine spark, hosted in the pineal gland, becomes the Pleroma, and the full Light of the Pleroma fills the entire body.

* * *

I see a large snake that stands vertically. It is as thick and as tall as a telegraph pole and towers above me. I think it is going to strike at me. My initial instinct is to retreat, but I realise I must confront it so turn and face it. I wait for it to strike, but rather than striking down at me, it moves towards, and into, me while remaining vertical. It merges with my spine and immediately blissful, energetic sensations run up and down my entire body. A brilliant white light radiates from between my eyes. It is so bright, I can barely look at it.

(Author's dream journal, September 2000)

I had this dream after watching the opening ceremony of the Sydney 2000 Olympic Games live on television. I was living in Sydney at the time and, in the lead up to the Games, was very much aware of the buzz around town. As a result, a certain amount of my attention was on the event, including its opening ceremony, and conditions were ripe for an activation within my psyche. The climax of the opening ceremony of any Olympic Games is always the lighting of the flame within the main stadium after the torch relay that brings the Olympic flame from Athens to the host city. When the torch entered

the stadium, it was passed between a number of Australia's most dec-
orated, and much loved, female Olympians, before being passed to
Cathy Freeman, an indigenous Australian (who, incidentally, went on
to win the gold medal in the women's 400 m athletics event, much
to the delight of the entire nation). Torch in hand, Freeman mounted
some kind of dais that had a surface layer of water. As she walked to
the centre of the dais, it appeared as if she was walking on water. From
there, she swept the torch in a circle around her feet, lighting a circle
of fire that then rose vertically with her in the centre. Once above her
head, the ring of fire connected with a near vertical ramp that was to
take it up to light the Olympic cauldron. However, it stalled at the
base of the ramp where it remained stuck for quite some time during
which, apparently, people worked out of sight to get it moving. Finally,
it started moving upwards, and the flame was lit. As I was watching
this I realised that the raising of what, in the East, is known as the
kundalini was being enacted symbolically. I also wondered if the stall-
ing of the fire represented the kundalini, generally, only making it
to the second chakra where it is lost in the sex act. Was this planned
as part of the ceremony? Divine intervention? Happenstance? Who
knows? This symbolism was enacted from a white man's perspective
in which it required a black woman, the opposite, to light the fire. Life
is born in the spark of opposites. I was also struck by the symbolism
in Freeman's name. Raising the kundalini to the third eye, where the
mystical marriage can be consummated, will *free man* (and woman).
This is the Gnostic resurrection.

* * *

The place where the spirit and soul meet in the imagination of the mind
is the *mundus imaginalis*, or the Imaginal World (Figure 21), a term first
proposed by the scholar and philosopher, Henri Corbin (1903–1978). For
Corbin, the *mundus imaginalis* is a very precise order of reality, which one
can engage with through visionary experience using the imagination,
and which corresponds to the *anima mundi*, the World Soul (Lachman,
2015). It consists of multiple worlds, each with its own landscape and
assortment of beings.

Like Jung's concept of the human mind as the gateway between the
outer and the inner, the *mundus imaginalis* exists both within and without. It is the world in which our dreams take place, or it can be engaged

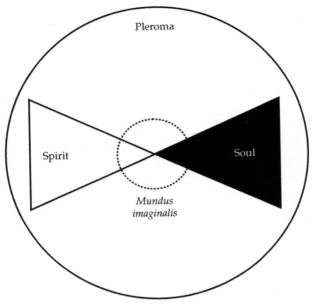

Figure 21. The *mundus imaginalis*. Spirit and soul meet in the *mundus imaginalis* which can be accessed via the imagination.

with more consciously through Jung's practice of active imagination. Corbin made the distinction between what he considered to be true imaginations from the imaginal realm, which he referred to as *imaginatio vera*, and personal fantasies in which we can create anything we desire to experience imaginatively (in the commonly used sense). Likewise, Jung stressed that during active imagination it is imperative to let the images of the unconscious speak for themselves, rather than allowing the ego to direct them, and risk the experience turning into mere fantasy. According to Lachman, by letting go of bodily sensations and entering into a meditative state, a voyager into the *mundus imaginalis* may encounter a supernatural being who will ask the voyager who she is and where she comes from. The voyager then replies that she is a traveller seeking to return to her true home, which lies beyond the world of the senses (2015, loc. 3488). Similarly, in *The Gospel of Thomas*, Christ teaches his disciples that if they are asked where they have come from, they are to reply that they have come from the light. It is through the intermediary realm of the *mundus imaginalis* that the Gnostic must pass during visionary ascension to the Pleroma.

With its strong emphasis on the role of the imagination, the Gnostic path is clearly an example of what is known as the *via positiva*. The *via positiva* is the practice of cataphatic theology (mentioned above) which attempts to access and experience the divine through images and symbols, and by way of ritual and other imaginative practices. On the other hand, the *via negativa*, the way of negation, is the practice of apophatic theology, which, in recognising the ineffable nature of the divine, dispenses with imagery and pursues pure contemplation of the divine. The *via negativa*, often referred to as the flight of the mystic, is the way of mysticism in which the mystic seeks union with the divine without concern for any intermediary realms that might exist between him, or her, and the object of contemplation. In contrast, the *via positiva*, within the Western Mystery Tradition, is the way of esotericism, in which the esotericist seeks to explore and understand the intermediary realm through the use of imagery and symbols, in other words, through the use of the imagination (ibid.). According to Lachman (2015), whereas the mystic seeks union with the divine, the esotericist is seeking knowledge, that is, gnosis, through the imagination. However, gnosis is not the goal of the Gnostic, it is only the means to the end, and is not sought for its own sake. The goal of the Gnostic is not the goal of the esotericist, but one and the same as the goal of the mystic. Like the mystic, the Gnostic seeks union with the divine which, in the words of the Gnostic, is a return to the Pleroma.

The Gnostic doctrine of the integration of opposites demands not the *via negativa or* the *via positiva*, but the *via negativa and* the *via positiva*. Once again, the Gnostic maxim of both/and rather than either/or. We might rephrase Jung's view that "We do not become enlightened by imagining figures of light, but only by bringing the darkness into the light of consciousness," into "We do not become enlightened by imagining figures of light *alone*, but by *also* bringing the darkness into the light of consciousness." The Pleroma is both the fullness and the emptiness, and the return to the Pleroma requires both the path of fullness, the *via positiva* (full of images), and the *via negativa* (devoid of images). We might consider the *via negativa* as the path of the spirit, and the *via positiva* as the path of the soul. Whereas the *via negativa* looks upward to receive the emissary from the realm of light, ultimately seeking union in the spiritual realms, the *via positiva* delves into the unconscious to rediscover the soul, by resolving opposites within the psyche through the use of the imagination. Both approaches are required. The practice of the *via positiva* to the exclusion of the *via negativa* leads to spiritual bypassing (discussed above); the *via negativa* without the *via positiva* leads to a psychologically well-adjusted person who remains an inmate of the Black Iron Prison.

In neither his *Exegesis* nor in the *Tractates* did PKD articulate a clear method for acquiring gnosis and effecting a return to the Pleroma. Waiting for a dark-haired young woman, with a fish pendant that fires pink beams of light, to come knocking on our door might not do the trick for the rest of us. Even if she does show up, and even if we get a flash of the pink light, there is no guarantee that it will trigger anamnesis in us. Jung, on the other hand, was quite methodical in articulating a modern method of Gnostic psycho-spiritual development—although he might never have admitted to it being described as such. This method is, of course, the process of individuation. In essence, individuation involves the reconciliation and integration of opposites through the transcendent function (see above) which leads to a higher state of consciousness. Holding the tension of the opposites that occur in the psyche when a conscious position is compensated by an unconscious counter-position creates an energy potential that generates the transcendent function which, in turn, propels consciousness to a higher level, and back towards the Pleroma. However, rather than a one-time event, it is an accumulation of marginal gains over a lifetime of practice. Psycho-spiritual development is complete when all opposites have been integrated and a state of psychic wholeness, the realisation of the Self, has been attained. When the perfect, harmonious balance of the opposites is achieved, when the mystical marriage of the bride and bridegroom is consummated, and when Christ and Sophia are reunited into the Christ-Sophia syzygy that mirrors the Mother-Father, and the One Self has been realised, then the dream is over, the created world ceases to exist, and we have returned home to the Pleroma. This is the Gnostic resurrection. The light and the dark can put their feet up, share a beer, and watch the sun go down. ... or else, the One Mind will have another dream, and the cosmic chess game between black and white begins again.

CHAPTER FOURTEEN

Reluctant gnosis

This work concludes with a creative synthesis resulting from this exploration of the gnosis of the reluctant Gnostics C. G. Jung and P. K. Dick. The use of the term "creative synthesis" in this instance simply acknowledges the fact that it is highly subjective. In homage to the inspired mind of PKD, it is presented in the style of his *Tractates* (although I've refrained from giving it any fancy Latin title).

1. Void and unknowable, the Pleroma is the ineffable nothingness before the beginning. It is neither created, nor not-created. It is non-being beyond being. It is the Godhead rather than God. The Pleroma is both the emptiness and the fullness. It has no qualities, yet it contains all qualities.

2. The Pleroma is fully transcendent and fully immanent. In the same way that light pervades the atmosphere, the Pleroma interpenetrates and pervades the created world. Split a piece of wood, or lift up a stone, and there will be found the Pleroma. Any distinction between the Pleroma and the created world is one of quality; the essence of the Pleroma is in the created world. There is no spatio-temporal separation.

3. *Barbelo* is the highest female principle. The Pleroma thinks, and his first thought, known as forethought, comes into being as Barbelo, his feminine counterpart, the first emanation and foremost of the aeons. One becomes Two as the Mother-Father. She is the creative power and the universal womb out of which everything else proceeds.

4. To assign gender to the One, the Pleroma, is incorrect. There can be no male without female; no female without male. The One, on its own, cannot have gender. Gender only arises when the One becomes Two.

5. Through the power of the Mother-Father, out of the emptiness of the Pleroma, the fullness of the Pleroma came into being through the emanation of male/female binary opposites known as syzygies. Individually, these emanated beings are the aeons. The last of these aeons is Sophia, Holy Wisdom, who forms a syzygy with her consort, Christ.

6. Creation occurred due to a primordial schism in which the perfect harmony of the primal syzygies was ruptured. If the primal syzygies had remained in perfect balance, unity would have persisted and the manifest universe could not have come into being. Creation *required* the harmonious balance to be disturbed and, as a result, disorder is not merely an unfortunate by-product of creation but one of the fundamental principles on which it is founded.

7. Creation is the result of the differentiation of pairs of binary opposites out of the Pleroma. Differentiation *is* creation. Without the differentiation of the opposites, there can be no world. Without differentiation, the syzygies of the Pleroma remain inert and *in potentia* only. Nothing can exist without the simultaneous existence of his complementary opposite. No hot without cold, no light without dark. In the Pleroma, prior to differentiation the opposites cancel one another out and are ineffective and not "real". If they can be considered to exist at all in the Pleroma, then the opposites exist in a harmonious state of equilibrium. Only once differentiated do they come into effect and become what might be considered as "real".

8. Life is born of the spark of opposites. Differentiation separates the opposites so that the resulting energy tension between the poles allows creation to come into being. Nothing can exist without a balancing opposite. Without differentiation, creation is an inherent potential of the Pleroma only, and the opposites remain in a state of perfect equilibrium. The created world is predicated on the differentiation of the opposites. This is the crux of Gnostic cosmogony.

9. Both/and rather than either/or. This is a Gnostic maxim. The opposites are not just part of life in this world, they are fundamental to it. No opposites, no world.

10. Non-differentiation of the opposites is unconsciousness; differentiation of the opposites is consciousness. If the opposites are not differentiated psychologically, a person risks the sin of unconsciousness. The reconciliation and integration of the fully differentiated opposites leads to psychological wholeness.

11. There is great danger in favouring one pole of a pair of opposites over its complementary opposite pole. Psychologically, an imbalance of the opposites results in a split in the psyche and a loss of psychological wholeness. The two poles of a pair of opposites may appear phenomenally distinct, but their essence is fundamentally one. The nature of the opposites in creation is differentiated-yet-inextricably-united. There is no hot without cold, no light without dark. Ultimately, the opposites can never be truly separated, they issue from a single root. The opposites are only meaningful in relation to one another. The essential nature of the opposites is always both/and rather than either/or. The glass is, simultaneously, both half empty and half full. We cannot have one pole of a pair of opposites without the other, and to the extent that we strive exclusively for one pole, we unavoidably fall under the spell of its counterpart. The rejected pole is forced down into the unconscious where it coalesces with the shadow, our own personal demiurge. Psychological wholeness demands the acceptance of both poles. We must walk the middle path between the opposites, being neither too attached, nor averse, to either pole. Both/and rather than either/or.

12. An imbalanced conscious position will invoke a compensatory unconscious counter-position due to the self-regulatory nature of the psyche. If the inner psychological state is not made conscious, in other words, if the conscious and unconscious counter-poles are not reconciled, then, out of necessity, the unresolved conflict will be encountered in the outer world in what is generally regarded as fate.

13. Enamoured by the Light of the Pleroma, Sophia wanted to conceive on her own. Striving only for the light evoked a counter-position of darkness. That darkness is the demiurge and the archons and their fallen creation. The demiurge, accompanied by his archons, is the blind, ignorant, dark abyss of the shadow of the Soul.

14. The demiurge and the archons are illegitimate. They are defective, and represent the disruption to the harmonious balance of the opposites that occurred in the Pleroma when Sophia conceived without her male counterpart. The archons are hermaphroditic. They are both male and female, yet not fully either. The harmony of the male/female syzygy has been disturbed within the archons, and the opposites are beginning to split. The archons are responsible for the severing of the original androgynous unity of the Pleroma into the duality of the created world. Having been created by the offspring of the last aeon, Sophia, the archons are far removed from the source of the Pleroma, and inhabit a liminal space within its lowest reaches, just on the cusp of the created world. As a result, the archons encroach upon, and have effect in, our world. This world is the dwelling place of many archons.

15. The demiurge, and his archons, lacked the power to create on their own. They hijacked the creative power of Barbelo, via her daughter Sophia, the demiurge's mother, in order to fashion the created world. The demiurge and the archons then created humanity in order to provide them with what they lacked, the Light of the Pleroma. They created humanity so that the Light of God reflected in humanity could illuminate them. In other words, the archons created humanity as an energy source. *The archons are energy parasites who feed off us!*

16. The archons' powers are limited. It is a mistake to think that the archons have power over us. They cannot overpower the truth. The archons have soul, and what is of soul cannot take hold of spirit. They can enact their violence on our bodies, minds, and souls, but they cannot harm our spirit. The spirit, on the other hand, is immaculate, immune, incorruptible, and immortal.

17. Due to their limited powers, the archons control humanity through deception. They do this in order to take free people and enslave them. Their power is their deception. The power of the archons is mere occlusion of the truth.

18. We are the archons. Sophia sent her daughter Zoe (meaning Life) into each one of us granting us a living soul. She is our Mother, she is also mother to the demiurge. He is our half-brother and, along with his offspring the archons, he is our collective shadow. All humans are archons, but some humans are more archonic than others.

19. Abraxas is the god-above-god that humanity has disavowed. He is two-natures-in-one, embodying both good and evil, God and devil. Anything real casts a shadow that is as great as itself, and the shadow of God is the devil. There cannot be one without the other. Both/and rather than either/or.

20. Created as much as creator, Abraxas is distinct from the Pleroma, yet cannot be wholly identified with the world either. Like the archons, Abraxas exists in the liminal space between the Pleroma and creation. Abraxas is the demiurge.

21. Abraxas is nothing and everything, eternal emptiness and eternal fullness, eternal darkness and eternal brightness, above and below, old and young, yes and no. However, unlike the syzygies of the Pleroma, in which the opposites cancel one another out, God and devil stand opposed to one another within the figure of Abraxas. Effectiveness is both the differentiator, and the connecting link, that unites God and devil in the figure of Abraxas. The effectiveness of Abraxas gives both God and devil the ability to have effect in the created world. To encounter Abraxas is to experience the numinous, the *mysterium tremendum et fascinans*, in all its awful mystery.

22. With the head of a rooster, a human body, and the tail of a snake, Abraxas unites the opposites, God and devil, good and evil, Heaven and Earth; opposites which collide in the experience of being human.

23. Given that he is two-natures-in-one, both God and devil, Abraxas is to not to be feared or loved, yet both feared and loved. Yet, he is neither to be sought after nor rejected since, like the archons' veil of deception, Abraxas surrounds us on all sides and will seek us out. We must walk the middle path between the opposites, being neither too attached, nor averse, to either pole. Both/and rather than either/or.

24. In the same way that the aeons and archons constitute the fullness of the Pleroma, the archetypes constitute the collective unconscious. The collective unconscious—and the archetypes—is, in *essence*, one and the same thing as the fullness of the Pleroma. The archetypes have their positive and negative aspects, and are thus capable of exerting both beneficial and/or detrimental effects. Thus, as their metaphysical counterparts, the aeons and the archons can influence the human psyche, indirectly shaping, if not controlling, human

experience. Psychologically, the archons are the negative aspects of the archetypes. It was the archons who compelled St. Paul against his will: "For that which I do I allow not: for what I would, that do I not; but what I hate, that do I. ... For the good that I would I do not: but the evil which I would not, that I do" (Romans 7:15–19, KJV).

25. Humanity has been imprisoned in the material world by the archons through an act of deception. This world is the Black Iron Prison. It is the shadow of death in which the human body is a tomb. This body-tomb has been created from the archons' four elements of: matter, darkness, desire, and the artificial spirit respectively. The human soul, trapped in a body-tomb, has been bound by the veil of forgetfulness, and enslaved in the material world. How has the great wealth of the human spirit come to dwell in the poverty of the body-tomb?

26. This world is an illusory dream world that we have been deceived into taking for reality. So-called reality is an illusion, albeit a very persistent, archon-enforced one. We are controlled by the archons because they control the false reality we are living in. However, the archons are effectively powerless, and their power over us exists only to the extent that they can deceive us into thinking that the false reality is actually real. This dream world is "real" as long as it lasts. We need to awaken from this sleep of death.

27. When we awaken to the illusion of the prison world, then we are no longer at its mercy. It will no longer control us, we will have control over it. When we realise that this world is an illusion, we transcend its limitations and become co-creators of it.

28. The essence of the universe is information. It is not three-dimensional, it is outside space and time altogether. Our world is a mere phantasm, a fallen world, in which space and time are part of the delusion. We have been thrown into this world, and enslaved by an evil entity that projects information which we have been deluded into interpreting as our so-called reality. This world is nothing more than the misinterpretation of an underlying reality of which the essence is simply information.

29. We humans are co-creators, along with the archons, in creating this dream world. We hypostatise the information we are fed into the phenomenal world. We are forgetful cosmic co-creators who have become imprisoned in a universe of our own making without realising it. Our illusory world is a mass hallucination. We are the archons.

30. The phenomenal world does not exist. It is a three-dimensional holographic image, an illusion, generated from information, which we mistake for reality. Like the prisoners in Plato's cave who mistake the shadows cast on the cave wall for reality, we, likewise, mistake our holographic world as being real. Our world is nothing more than a satanic interpolation of underlying information that results in a prison which occludes the information that will reveal our true situation. The fundamental nature of the fullness of the Pleroma is energetic information, and the archons have distorted this underlying information to project the illusory world in which we are imprisoned.

31. The Pleroma consists of analogue waveforms (undifferentiated opposites), and the created world consists of binaries (differentiated opposites). The poles of the pairs of opposites within the Pleroma can oscillate instantaneously, such that the male is not male, and the female is not female, whereas the created world, brought into existence through conscious observation, is binary in that it requires the tension between the differentiated opposites to spark creation into existence.

32. "The kingdom of God is within you" (Luke 17:21, KJV). The innermost core of every human being is a divine spark of the Light of the Pleroma. The macrocosm is reflected in the microcosm, hence, we are within the Pleroma, and the Pleroma is also within us. The divine spark within is a fragment of the entire cosmic hologram, only dimmer. As a part of the Pleroma, the divine spark contains the entire Pleroma, only less so. The divine spark is the indwelling Christ. "In him dwelleth all the fullness of the [Pleroma] bodily" (Colossians 2:9, KJV).

33. Due to the archons, the divine spark has become estranged from the Pleroma and imprisoned in matter. We are divine sparks enclosed in corruptible sheaves. When the divine spark remembers itself as both a part, and yet the whole, of the Pleroma, this is *the* gnosis of the Gnostics.

34. Our essence is the divine spark. Spirit, the immaculate divine spark, is immortal. As a part of the hologram of the Pleroma, it is one with the Pleroma, and contains the fullness of the entire Pleroma, only dimmer.

35. Gnosis alone is not enough for salvation. Gnosis is imparted by the emissary who descends from the Pleroma to free humanity from its

imprisonment in the world of darkness. "I am the light of the world: he that followeth me shall not walk in darkness, but shall have the light of life" (John 8:12, KJV).

36. The Self is the unifying and ordering centre of the whole psyche. The Self is the psychological aspect of the Christ, and the Christ is the spiritual aspect of the Self. They are one and the same at different dimensions of being. Realisation of the Self is the goal of life. It demands the reconciliation and integration of all opposites within the psyche, principal among them the union of the conscious and unconscious psyches.

37. The emissary can come as an image of the Self from the depths of the unconscious. The emissary from above, and the Self from below, are one and the same. The Pleroma and the collective unconscious are One.

38. There is only One Self. My Self is your Self; they are one and the same. One Mind there is; One Self there is, and that One Self is the fullness of the Pleroma.

39. The Self is Christ is the divine spark. The fully realised Christ manifests the full Light of the Pleroma.

40. Know thy Self. Be thy Self. Express thy Self. Creativity is freedom; conformity is slavery.

41. The emissary is known as the *plasmate*, an immortal form of energy which is living information. Through a process of cross-bonding, the plasmate can unite with a human being such that the human is permanently annexed to the plasmate, resulting in a *homoplasmate*, a divine-human syzygy. Cross-bonding is the reunion with the male plasmate with a female host and occurs in the pineal gland.

42. We are one with God, we are the creator, and we are the archons. We are also the saviour, and the one who needs to be saved; not two, but one. *Salvador salvandus*. We are one with the Pleroma. We are the Pleroma. It is in us, and we are in it. Collectively, we are the One. Individually, we are a microcosm of the One. This is the gnosis of PKD.

43. The spirit is wholly of the Pleroma. The body is wholly of the world of matter. The soul is dual in nature: the divine aspect, or the living soul, that comes from Sophia, and the material aspect, or animal soul, that comes from the archons. The soul animates the body, and the spirit vivifies the soul. Without spirit, the soul is a lifeless soul.

44. When the divine harmony was ruptured and the twin poles (male/ female) of the original androgynous unity were split apart and man- ifested in matter, they lost their spiritual nature and were reduced to a lower level of existence, the archonic, animal soul level. The reunion of spirit and the living soul, the restoration of the primal syzygy, generates life. Without reunion both twins of the syzygy are lacking their spiritual essence, they are mere souls, and nothing more than the living dead. This is the crux of Gnostic soteriology.

45. While the purity of the primal male/female syzygy was intact, the soul remained whole and in the Pleroma. Due to the rupture of the syzygy, the primordial fall occurred and the soul fell down into a physical body and entered human existence. The fall is not being born in sin, it is the rupture of the male and the female unity. Having been separated for millennia, the male (spirit) and female (soul) halves of the Pleroma need to be reunited to restore the primordial unity.

46. In the world, the soul becomes seduced by the distractions of the material world. Materialism, physicality, and the pleasures of the senses become her masters and she their slave. Addicted to the pas- sions of the psyche and the flesh, she is trapped in the world of shadows. She needs to reject her "whoring" and, once cleansed, will be rejuvenated as a living soul.

47. Like Sophia without her male counterpart, the soul is unable to conceive on her own and needs her male counterpart. Being only one twin of a pair of opposites, the soul is unable to engender life. Her polar opposite is required and so her consort is sent down from the Pleroma into the whoredom of the realm of matter to rescue the fallen soul who is imprisoned by the archons. Her saviour, the "bridegroom", and the soul, the "bride", must be reunited in the mystical marriage in the bridal chamber. This is the resurrection from the dead, freedom from captivity in the world of matter, and the return to the Pleroma. Animal souls who are enslaved by their addictions to the distractions of the world, and who prostitute themselves to them, bar themselves from the rite of the mystical marriage. Only those who have freed themselves from the bonds of physicality and attained the purity of the living spirit can enter the bridal chamber.

48. We *are* spirit, we *have* soul. The soul knows duality. It must make a choice. The red pill or the blue pill. The whoredom of the animal

soul in our brothel world, giving itself over to the passions of the mind and of the flesh, or seeking its redemption, its reunion with spirit, and a return to the purity of the realm of Light.

49. The psychological counterpart of spirit and soul is the anima/animus complex which functions as the interface to the inner world of the unconscious. It acts as a bridge between the outer and inner worlds, and facilitates a dialogue between the ego and the Self, the image of God within the unconscious. The anima/animus is the doorway into the depths of the psyche. The relationship between the ego and the anima/animus archetype within the unconscious is characterised by the male/female polarity of the self-regulating psyche. To the extent that the ego identifies with the masculine pole, the anima/animus adopts a compensatory feminine nature, and similarly, to the extent that the ego identifies as feminine, the anima/animus will appear masculine.

50. Spirituality and sexuality are a pair of opposites. They are not just *a* pair of opposites, but from a human perspective, *the* essential pair of opposites. The world comes into being through the differentiation of opposites in which the tension between the differentiated poles generates the necessary energy potential that gives rise to creation. It is only through the interplay of the cosmic forces of spirituality and sexuality that humanity can come into being. It is *only* within humanity that the interaction between spirituality, symbolised by a bird, and sexuality, symbolised by a serpent, can occur, hence the figure of Abraxas, who epitomises the clash of opposites, displays the bird-human-serpent symbolism.

51. In Jung's gnosis, the sexuality of the male principle is more earthly and descends, whereas that of the feminine is more spiritual and ascends. In contrast, the spirituality of the male is more heavenly, and is oriented upwards towards the infinite, whereas the spirituality of the feminine is more earthly and is oriented towards the finite. The celestial mother governs female spirituality and male sexuality, whereas the earthly father governs male spirituality and female sexuality. In other words, the male and female principles are dual-natured and within each pole of the male/female polarity there exists a spirituality/sexuality polarity with different, but complementary, governing principles. This polarity within a polarity serves to illustrate the dynamic nature of the opposites in the Pleroma in which the twin poles within any given syzygy

have not been differentiated. Like an alternating voltage in electrical systems, in which the voltage reverses direction periodically, the twin poles within the syzygy can switch their polarity, one moment male, female the next, and vice versa.

52. The only goal of the Gnostic is to return to the Pleroma. Salvation is the liberation of the divine spark from the spatio-temporal, material prison world, and its reinstatement to the realm of light, or into the depth and silence. Whereas the Neoplatonist might seek a return to the One, the Gnostic seeks a return to the Zero, in other words, the Nothingness of the Pleroma.

53. When the bride and bridegroom come together in the mystical marriage there is only one name for their union and that is rest; the rest that results from nothing but the pure contemplation of the divine. "Come unto me, all ye that labour and are heavy laden, and I will give you rest" (Matthew 11:28, KJV).

54. The resurrection and return to the original purity of the Pleroma, dependent on salvific gnosis, includes the realisation that our spiritual essence is something that we already possess. It is not something that we need to develop, it is something we need to realise. We are already of the Pleroma, in the Pleroma, and permeated by the Pleroma. The resurrection is anamnesis of our divine heritage.

55. The return to the Pleroma is a contemplative journey involving a visionary ascent through a series of inner planes. These planes are controlled by the archons and must be carefully navigated in order to evade the archons who will do what they can to thwart the Gnostic's efforts and keep him, or her, enslaved in the lower realms. The "ascent" is metaphorical, and not a movement upwards. It is the expansion of consciousness and an increase in gnosis.

56. These visionary ascents are not one-off events in which gnosis is acquired in the mother of all mystical experiences. They are, typically, brief events which provide a foretaste of the ultimate ascent the soul will make following the death of the body. Before visionary ascent, chop wood and carry water; after visionary ascent, chop wood and carry water. The attainment of gnosis is a process of incremental gains over a lifetime of dedicated practice. After each partial trip up the mountain to render unto God what is God's, the Gnostic practitioner returns, with a little more gnosis, to the world and, out of necessity due to the limits of the body, to the task of rendering unto Caesar, while preparing for the next attempt at the summit.

57. Crucial to the resurrection is the need to both a) reconcile the opposites, and b) realise the ultimate dissolution of the opposites in the
Pleroma. If one is whole, then one will be filled with light, but if
one is divided, then one will be filled with darkness. When one has
integrated the opposites, when the bride and bridegroom have consummated their mystical marriage in the bridal chamber, then one
will be filled with the light of the Pleroma. As long as the opposites are differentiated, and the bride has forsaken her betrothed
and continues whoring, one remains condemned to the darkness of
the world.

58. One will only return to the Pleroma when the two are made into one,
when upper and lower are reconciled, and when the male and the
female are reunited into a single being so that their gender differentiation is dissolved. Then, and only then, will the Gnostic see the
light of the Pleroma. The return to the primal unity of the Pleroma
is premised on the balancing of the opposites. The return, like the
beginning, is unitary where there is neither male nor female, and all
syzygies exist in a perfect state of harmonious equipoise, no movement, no vibration, no sound, just silence.

59. Those who do not fast from the world will not find the Kingdom
of Heaven. Only someone who completely renounces the things
of the world and subdues the passions can realise the truth of
God. The power of the pure intercourse of the mystical marriage,
which occurs in a realm superior to this one, has become defiled
in its image on Earth, the carnal marriage. Only one who accomplishes the rite of the mystical marriage will receive the holy light,
and if it is not received in this realm, it cannot be received in any
other place.

60. Salvation requires a growth in consciousness in this life. Humanity's worst sin is unconsciousness. Differentiation of the opposites
is what saves humanity from unconsciousness. Consciousness
demands the differentiation of opposites, and growth in consciousness demands the reconciliation and integration of the opposites.
Psychologically, the struggle for salvation does not pit aeons against
archons, but occurs in the unconscious, where psychic factors that
will save us are opposed by psychic factors that will condemn us.

61. Salvation means escape from this world, the Black Iron Prison, in
which our minds have been deliberately occluded to blind us to the
fact of our imprisonment. The key to salvation is not to give in to

what would be a natural urge to fight the system. What we resist, persists. Those who fight against the Empire become the Empire. To the extent we defeat the Empire, we become the Empire. We are the Empire and the Black Iron Prison. We are the jailed and our own jailers. We are the archons. All humans are archons, but some humans are more archonic than others.

62. Gnosis is direct, unmediated, experience *of* the divine, in distinction to someone else's doctrine *about* the divine. Gnosis is the only road to salvation; ignorance and unconsciousness is sin.

63. Gnosis is revealed in secret. When you pray, enter into the silence of your heart, and pray to your Mother-Father who is in secret.

64. Second only to the conscious/unconscious polarity, there is no pair of opposites in greater need of our urgent attention than the primal syzygy, the male/female dichotomy. It is impossible to become whole when one half of that whole, the feminine, is denied. Critical to the salvation of humanity is the restoration of the divine feminine.

65. The union of spirit and the living soul occurs in the mirrored bridal chamber. Spirit and the living soul are mirror images of one another and have equal status. Spiritual practice aimed at receiving the spirit must be complemented by work to reclaim the soul.

66. Preparing the bride to receive the bridegroom means reconnecting with, and recovering, one's lost soul. The reclamation of the soul requires a descent into the chthonic depths of the unconscious. Only to the extent that a tree's roots dig down into the earth, can its branches reach to the heavens. Without the roots, there can be no branches reaching up to Heaven. The roots come first. In order to ascend, we must first descend. Authentic spirituality must be founded on a psychology that realises the soul and works to liberate the living soul from the imprisonment in the world of the animal soul. The bridegroom will only appear to the extent that the bride has been prepared.

67. Whoever is near to the saviour is near to the fire. To realise the reunion of spirit and soul necessitates that one endures the fire. It is incumbent upon every true Gnostic to burn away all that gets in the way of liberating the living soul. Only to the extent that we descend into the unconscious and expose ourselves over and over to the annihilation of the animal soul can we recover the lost living soul.

68. One cannot attain the light above without first addressing the demons in the darkness of the depths, that is, by bringing the darkness into the light of consciousness. Preparing the bride, recovering the soul, requires working with the darkness of the unconscious. The living soul can only be reclaimed by delving into the shadowy depths of the unconscious, and this rescue mission means addressing our demons and wrestling with the darkness that holds her captive.

69. Recovering the living soul demands that we address not only our personal shadow, but also the darkness of the collective, demiurgic shadow to the extent that it touches us. As long as the root of evil remains hidden, its power over us will persist. It is powerful because we do not recognise it. When it is brought into the light of consciousness, it dies. As long as it is ignored, it takes root in our heart and dominates us. We become its slaves. If we are not conscious of the archons within us, they fall into the shadow. Liberating the soul begins with recognising the darkness.

70. Christ is a male/female, Christ/Sophia, syzygy. This realisation is the restoration of Sophia. Two essences in one.

71. Imagination is the only weapon in the war against the false reality imposed by the archons.

72. It is neither the soul nor the spirit that sees visions, but the mind, through the faculty of the imagination. The imagination can take us anywhere, up there, in here, or down there, and it is through the imagination that the above and below, the inner and outer, the spirit and the soul, and the Pleroma and the created world, can be reconciled and integrated. The imagination is the means of our salvation. Only in the imagination of the human mind, poised between the opposites, can the integration and dissolution of the opposites be accomplished.

73. *You* do not create your own reality, collectively, *we* create your reality. Collectively, we dream our so-called reality into existence. However, we are the archons—as well as the archons' slaves—and it is our minds, under the influence of our archonic selves, that are continuously dreaming this prison world into existence. We need to dream a better dream, and quickly.

74. Humanity is the interface between two worlds. The upper world of the bird and the lower world of the serpent only meet within humanity. The tension of the opposites between the upper and lower

worlds brings creation into existence. In order to become we have to undergo the battle between the bird and the serpent. Human existence occurs in the middle world where the opposites of bird and serpent are pitted against one another.

75. The images from the unconscious, mediated by the imagination, are the means by which the truth is perceived.

76. The Pleroma will only be realised when the inner and the outer, and the upper and the lower, and the male and the female, have been integrated so that no distinction exists between them. The place where they meet and the integration takes place is in the human. The reunion of spirit and soul, through the imagination, occurs only in the human who has realised Christ. Only when the bride has been prepared by elevating the soul from an animal soul to a living soul, and the bridegroom, the emissary from the Pleroma with its salvific gnosis, has been received, can the mystical marriage be consummated by the power of the imagination. For the Gnostic, this is Christ-realisation, the way, the truth, and the life, without which no one returns to the Pleroma.

77. The archons cannot see a person who wears the perfect light, and cannot prevent that person's ascension. This body of light is created in the mystery of union. Only once spirit and soul are reunited in the bridal chamber does the Gnostic don the garment of perfect light that protects him, or her, from the archons during the ascent back to the Pleroma. The bridal chamber, where the mystical marriage takes place, is located in the pineal gland. "The light of the body is the eye: if therefore thine eye be single, thy whole body shall be full of light" (Matthew 6:22, KJV). When the mystical union occurs in the third eye, then the divine spark, hosted in the pineal gland, becomes the Pleroma, and the full Light of the Pleroma fills the entire body.

78. The Gnostic path is, primarily, the *via positiva*. However, the integration of opposites demands both the *via negativa and* the *via positiva*. Both/and rather than either/or. The *via negativa* is the path of spirit, the *via positiva* is the path of the soul. We do not become enlightened by imagining figures of light *alone*, but by *also* bringing the darkness into the light of consciousness. The Pleroma is both the fullness and the emptiness, and the return to the Pleroma requires both the path of fullness, the *via positiva* (full of images), and the *via negativa* (devoid of images).

79. Psychologically, the reconciliation and integration of opposites involves holding the tension of the opposites, which occur in the psyche when a conscious position is compensated by an unconscious counter-position, until the resultant energy potential evokes the transcendent function which propels consciousness to a higher level and back towards the Pleroma.

80. Psycho-spiritual development is complete when all opposites have been integrated and a state of psychic wholeness, the realisation of the Self, has been attained. When the perfect, harmonious balance of the opposites is achieved, when the mystical marriage of the bride and bridegroom is consummated, then Christ and Sophia are reunited and the One Self has been realised, the dream is over, the created world ceases to exist, and we have returned home to the Pleroma. This is the Gnostic resurrection.

REFERENCES

Barnstone, W., & Meyer, M. (Eds.) (2003). *The Gnostic Bible*. Boston, MA: New Seeds.

Brakke, D. (2010). *The Gnostics: Myth, Ritual, and Diversity in early Christianity* [Kindle version]. Retrieved from www.amazon.com

Castaneda, C. (2017). The words of Don Juan Matus. Retrieved January 23, 2017 from https://archive.org/stream/CarlosCastanedaTheWords OfDonJuanMatus/Carlos%20Castaneda-The%20Words%20Of%20 Don%20Juan%20Matus_djvu.txt

Chödrön, P. (2000). *When Things Fall Apart: Heart Advice for Difficult Times*. Boulder, CO: Shambhala.

Churton, T. (2015). *Gnostic Mysteries of Sex: Sophia the Wild One and Erotic Christianity* [Kindle version]. Retrieved from www.amazon.com

Comella, P. (2014). *The Collapse of Materialism: Visions of Science, Dreams of God* [Kindle version]. Retrieved from www.amazon.com

Daumal, R. (2017). *René Daumal Quotes*. Retrieved August 16, 2017 from https://www.goodreads.com/author/quotes/3020747.Ren_Daumal

Dick, P. K. (1977). If you find this world bad, you should see some of the others. Retrieved April 30, 2016 from https://ia600500.us.archive.org/ 32/items/PhilipKDickSpeechExcerpts/PhilipKDick_Speech.txt

Dick, P. K. (1978). How to build a universe that doesn't fall apart two days later. Retrieved January 15, 2016 from http://deoxy.org/pkd_how2-build.htm

Dick, P. K. (2001). *VALIS*. London: Orion.

Dick, P. K. (2008). *The Divine Invasion*. London: Harper Voyager.

Dick, P. K. (2011). *The Exegesis of Philip K. Dick* [Kindle version]. Retrieved from www.amazon.com

Douglas, S. (2016). *White Bird, Black Serpent, Red Book: Exploring the Gnostic Roots of Jungian Psychology through Dreamwork*. London: Karnac.

Eliot, T. S. (1943). *Four Quartets*. Retrieved August 15, 2017 from https://genius.com/Ts-eliot-four-quartets-little-gidding-annotated

Ellis, N. (2012). *Imagining the World into Existence: An Ancient Egyptian Manual of Consciousness* [Kindle version]. P. Jackson & J. Lethem (Eds.). Retrieved from www.amazon.com

Fosella, T., & Welwood, J. (2011). Human nature, Buddha nature: An interview with John Welwood. *Tricycle: The Buddhist Review, 20*(3).

Griffiths, B. (1982). *The Marriage of East and West*. Springfield, IL: Templegate.

Hart, T., Nelson. P. L., & Puhakka, K. (2000). *Transpersonal Knowing: Exploring the Horizon of Consciousness*. Albany, NY: State University of New York Press.

Hoeller, S. A. (2002a). *Gnosticism: New Light on the Ancient Tradition of Inner Knowing*. Wheaton, IL: Theosophical.

Hoeller, S. A. (2002b). *The Gnostic Jung and the Seven Sermons to the Dead*. Wheaton, IL: Theosophical.

Jung, C. G. (1951). Aion: Researches into the phenomenology of the self. In: G. Adler, M. Fordham, & H. Read (Series Eds.), R. F. C. Hull (Trans.), *The Collected Works of C. G. Jung, Vol. 9: Part 2*. Princeton, NJ: Princeton University Press, 1959.

Jung, C. G. (1954). Psychological commentary on "The Tibetan Book of the Great Liberation". In: *Psychology and the East* (pp. 103–137). London: Ark, 1978.

Jung, C. G. (1955–1956). *Mysterium coniunctionis: An Inquiry into the Separation and Synthesis of Psychic Opposites in Alchemy*. In: G. Adler, M. Fordham, & H. Read (Series Eds.), R. F. C. Hull (Trans.), *The Collected Works of C. G. Jung: Vol. 14*. Princeton, NJ: Princeton University Press, 1963.

Jung, C. G. (1957a). Psychological commentary on "The Tibetan Book of the Dead". In: *Psychology and the East* (pp. 59–76). London: Ark, 1978.

Jung, C. G. (1957b). The transcendent function. In: J. Chodorow (Ed.), *Jung on Active Imagination* (pp. 42–60). Princeton, NJ: Princeton University Press, 1997.

Jung, C. G. (1962). *Memories, Dreams, Reflections*. London: Fontana, 1995.

Jung, C. G. (1973). Letter to Smith. In: G. Adler (Ed.), R. F. C. Hull (Trans.), *C. G. Jung Letters, Vol. II, 1951–1961* (pp. 570–573). Princeton, NJ: Princeton University Press.

Jung, C. G. (2009). *The Red Book: Liber Novus. A Reader's edition.* Edited and with an introduction by S. Shamdasani. M. Kyburz, J. Peck; S. Shamdasani (Trans.). New York: W. W. Norton.

Kastrup, B. (2011). *Dream Up Reality: Diving into the Mind to Uncover the Astonishing Hidden Tale of Nature* [Kindle version]. Retrieved from www. amazon.com

Kastrup, B. (2015). *Brief Peeks Beyond: Critical Essays on Metaphysics, Neuroscience, Free Will, Scepticism and Culture* [Kindle version]. Retrieved from www.amazon.com

Kastrup, B. (2016). Quantum physics meets mythology: Going forward by taking a step back. *New Dawn Special Issue, 10*(4).

Lachman, G. (2015). *The Secret Teachers of the Western World* [Kindle version]. Retrieved from www.amazon.com

Lash, J. L. (2006). *Not in His Image: Gnostic Vision, Sacred Ecology, and the Future of Belief.* White River Junction, VT: Chelsea Green.

Lewis, N. D. (2013). *Introduction to Gnosticism: Ancient Voices, Christian Worlds.* New York: Oxford University Press.

Madden, K. W. (2008). *Dark Light of the Soul.* Great Barrington, MA: Lindisfarne.

Masters, R. A. (2016). *Spiritual Bypassing: Avoidance in Holy Drag.* Retrieved December 18, 2016 from http://robertmasters.com/writings/spiritual-bypassing/

Matrix, The (1999). J. Silver (producer), A. Wachowski, A. & L. Wachowski (directors). Warner Bros motion picture.

McGuire, W., & Shamdasani, S. (Eds.) (2012). *Introduction to Jungian Psychology: Notes of the Seminar on Analytical Psychology Given in 1925.* Princeton, NJ: Princeton University Press.

Meyer, M. (Ed.) (2007). *The Nag Hammadi Scriptures: The Revised and Updated Translation of Sacred Gnostic Texts.* New York: HarperCollins.

Peake, A. (2013). *A Life of Philip K. Dick: The Man Who Remembered the Future* [Kindle version]. Retrieved from www.amazon.com

Pearson, B. A. (2007). *Ancient Gnosticism: Traditions and Literature* [Kindle version]. Retrieved from www.amazon.com

Plotinus. *The Six Enneads.* S. MacKenna & B. S. Page (Trans.). Grand Rapids, MI: Christian Classics Ethereal Library, 2017. Retrieved August 24, 2017 from http://www.ccel.org/ccel/plotinus/enneads.pdf

Plotkin, B. (2003). *Soulcraft: Crossing into the Mysteries of Nature and Psyche.* Novato, CA: New World Library.

Rosenblum, B., & Kuttner, F. (2012). *Quantum Enigma: Physics Encounters Consciousness* [Kindle version]. Retrieved from www.amazon.com

Rowan, J. (2005). *The Transpersonal: Spirituality in Psychotherapy and Counselling (2nd ed.)*. London: Routledge.

Rudolph, K. (1987). *Gnosis: The Nature and History of Gnosticism*. R. M. Wilson (Trans.). New York: Harper San Francisco.

Ruumet, H. (2006). *Pathways of the Soul: Exploring the Human Journey*. Victoria, BC, Canada: Trafford.

Scopello, M. (2007). Introduction to the exegesis on the soul. In: M. Meyer (Ed.), *The Nag Hammadi Scriptures: The Revised and Updated Translation of Sacred Gnostic Texts* (pp. 223–226). New York: HarperCollins.

Sharp, D. (2010). *Jung Lexicon: A Primer of Terms & Concepts*. Retrieved April 30, 2016 from http://www.psychceu.com/jung/sharplexicon.html

Smith, A. P. (2008). *The Gnostics: History, Tradition, Scriptures, Influence*. London: Watkins.

Smoley, R. (2006). *Forbidden Faith: The Gnostic Legacy from the Gospels to the Da Vinci Code*. New York: HarperCollins.

Stein, M. (1998). *Jung's Map of the Soul* [Kindle version]. Retrieved from www.amazon.com

Stevenson, R. L. (1886). *The Strange Case of Dr. Jekyll and Mr. Hyde*. Retrieved August 16, 2017 from http://www.litcharts.com/lit/dr-jekyll-and-mr-hyde/quotes

Stratford, J. (2007). *Living Gnosticism: An Ancient Way of Knowing*. Berkeley, CA: Apocryphile Press.

Stein, M. (2014). *Minding the Self: Jungian Meditations on Contemporary Spirituality*. Hove, UK: Routledge.

Thomassen, E. (2007). Introduction to the treatise on resurrection. In: M. Meyer (Ed.), *The Nag Hammadi Scriptures: The Revised and Updated Translation of Sacred Gnostic Texts* (pp. 49–51). New York: HarperCollins.

Trainspotting (1996). A. Macdonald (producer), D. Boyle (director). Channel Four Films motion picture.

Turner, J. D. (2001). *Sethian Gnosticism and the Platonic Traditions*. Quebec, Canada: Les Presses de L'Université Laval.

Williams, M. A. (1996). *Rethinking Gnosticism: Arguments for Dismantling a Dubious Category*. Princeton, NJ: Princeton University Press.

INDEX

187